BOAT
CUISINE

BOAT
CUISINE

The all-weather cookbook

June Raper

fernhurst BOOKS

Copyright © Fernhurst Books 1994

First published as The Beaufort Scale Cookbook in 1989 by
Fernhurst Books, Duke's Path, High Street, Arundel, West Sussex
BN18 9AJ

Printed and bound in China through World Print

British Library Cataloguing in Publication Data:
A catalogue record for this book is available from the British Library.

ISBN 1-898660-02-6

Designed by Joyce Chester
Cover design by Simon Balley
Cover photograph by PPL
Typeset by Book Economy Services
www.fernhurstbooks.co.uk

Contents

Introduction by Delia Smith

I have had to cook meals in some pretty cramped and inconvenient places in my time but never, I confess, in a ship's galley. June Raper has, and for much of her married life. Not only has this made her a seasoned sailor, it has provided her with a wealth of recipes that can be cooked in anything from a gentle breeze to a force nine gale.

Naturally the emphasis is on practicality and safety, but not at the expense of taste. Getting back to harbour seven hours late because of a foul tide and hungry because you only had sandwiches for lunch is nothing short of self-flagellation!

Cooking afloat calls for ingenuity – not least when everything around you is swinging chaotically – and there is plenty of that in this book. You'd be amazed what can be rustled up in a pressure cooker or a pump action vacuum flask. I have no doubt that June's imaginative recipes and ideas can add a new and delicious dimension to your next voyage. Put a copy in the locker now!

Author's Acknowledgements

My gratitude is due to Delia Smith for allowing me to use the recipes included here from her *How to Cheat at Cooking*, and specially for kindly agreeing to write an introduction to this book. To the Delta Hotel, Vlaardingen, Rotterdam, for their recipes for celeriac, to the Norwegian Prawn Council for the recipes from their *Tasty Dishes with Norwegian Prawns*, and to John Tovey for allowing me to use his recipe for rough puff pastry, thank you. I am grateful to you all.

I am also grateful to Peggy Auger, Jean Burrells, Marion Campbell, Ruby Corke, David Cawthorne, Maureen Davie, Pat Ellis, Mary Gibson, Bess Hill, Maureen Hull, Linda Jensen, Yvonne Lloyd, Barbara Massey, Liz Price, Kay Raper, Shirley Raper, Catriona de Vere and Ann Wicking for sharing their favourite recipes with me and which I now pass on.

I would like to thank the following people for help in conversions, recipe testing and proof reading: Carole Harvey, Neville Rowan and Roger Towning; and a special thank-you to Grace Godino who has given me invaluable help with all these – particularly with the American names and conversion tables.

And finally my thanks to Bill for his help *when asked* and for keeping out of my way at other times and to our two children, Shirley and Christopher, for putting up with my 'concoctions' at sea for years. To my many friends not mentioned specifically whose brains I have picked shamelessly – bless you all.

June Raper
M.F.V. 'Ros Arcan'
Turkey

Cooking Afloat

I have found over my years of sailing that although there is no problem in cooking on a boat (even a small one) when the weather is fine and the sea smooth, it is a different ball-game when the wind comes up (we have a genius for finding strong head winds whichever direction we choose to take) and the boat begins to dance. The question arises of what can be made easily, without being below long enough to feel ill – and all good shore-side intentions flee. We usually ended up with cheese and biscuits or beans on toast. Interesting ideas were conspicuous by their absence! So, I began to look round for a book which would provide me with such ideas for simple meals (and save a divorce a week!).

Although there are books on how to cook delicious meals at sea, those I could find were written by intrepid sailors crossing oceans, or crewing on large yachts, obviously more competent or, to be honest, more enthusiastic in their sea-cooking than I. I quailed when confronted with remarks like 'how to make jam at sea' or 'take four pints of water and a lobster' and for years I remained in the same predicament – lots of food on board but without the inclination to think of *what* to concoct easily when the weather piped up or even when I was merely tired.

There is no escaping the fact that if you want a nourishing or hot meal it has to be prepared – somehow. But this can be made reasonably simple if one is armed with ideas suitable to the occasion.

We are now retired and cruising permanently and this has jogged me into rectifying the position for myself and also, I trust, for other seacooks in the same boat if you'll forgive the pun.

Perhaps it will be useful to those on long ocean crossings but it is intended primarily for those who sail at weekends, either round their own coasts, or to nearby countries; for those who like to spend their summer holidays on boats or for those who, like us, have time for an extended leisurely cruise, putting into port fairly regularly.

I do not believe there is room on a small boat for quantities of foodstuffs or that it is practical or economic to carry too much. It is more healthy and cheaper to buy as you go, keeping only basic items such as flour, sugar, cereals and some emergency rations on board for use when caught at sea longer than intended, or for those times when you just can't be bothered to prepare meals with fresh ingredients.

HINTS

Some of the following notes may seem basic, and so they are, but they may be helpful to those just starting out on their sailing lives, and so I make no excuses for stating the obvious. Some notes will be less so and I hope, helpful to many.

Points to remember when planning a meal:

● In heavy weather water rolls with the boat, so keep it minimal and cook in deep pans when possible. This applies even more so to hot oil, which should be avoided except in very small quantities. (Think how healthy that is too.)

● Be sure pans are firmly wedged somehow, and do not slide about. Most stoves have fiddles with a movable bar on top; do use it. In an emergency a piece of rubber-stretch cord with hooks (usually used for fastening sails or luggage) may be used, hooked onto the stove grid and over the pot. But there are two snags – look out for it coming into contact with the flame, and be careful it does not slip off the pot. If you have a handle on the pot lid with a space under it, put the cord through the hole; this will hold it in place.

● In heavy weather most crews want warm sustaining but attractive meals, so small touches and variety in simple meals are more important than fancy dishes which take all day to prepare. It is true that you eat with your eyes – a sprig of parsley, a prettily cut tomato or other garnish helps. They can be prepared beforehand and left in a plastic box.

● Look out the ingredients you require before you leave, or when it *begins* to look rough – and be sure they are well protected until required.

● Try to prepare as much as you can before you set out. This does mean a bit of pre-planning but it saves a frantic search for food when you are faced with a strong wind, or are tired after a long day on the beach. When ashore you never remember the weather being as bad as it is till the next time you are caught. If the weather turns out to be better than expected then the sea-cook who has prepared for the worst is all set to take things easy.

● Make a point of thinking about meals when safely anchored or at home and note down ideas: you'll never think of them with a crew clamouring for food in a force five headwind.

● Remember your 'kitchen' is now a 'galley' and never be fooled into thinking it is a safe, stable place because you are 'only out on the river'. As sure as splashes are splashes a fast launch will set you rolling just when you have all your ingredients about you and they will no longer be to hand but plastered over deck and bulkheads. Prepare things one by one and then be sure they are safely wedged while waiting to be used in the dish you are preparing.

● Avoid when possible meals involving filthy pans. If you can buy non-stick pans they are worth their cost. It's awful to leave the washing up till you 'get to port' or 'the weather improves' or even until the morning and be faced with a grim, greasy, cold, hard-to-clean pan; it is even less enjoyable trying to do it on the spot when tossing about.

● There are four items I'd hate to be without when sailing. The first is a non-stick milk pan (easily cleaned, all-purpose and conveniently deep). The second is a pressure cooker. The third item is a lidless kettle, filled through the spout, causing much less danger of spilled hot water. The fourth is a pump action vacuum flask which, again, avoids hot liquid spills.

● Keep clear of glass containers when possible. Write good labels – it is a good idea to mark tins in case you lose the labels through damp, rain or sea water. Marker pens work well.

● Make sure you have good catches on the

lockers or cupboards and your stores and equipment are well secured. There is nothing worse than scraping up a mess of chutney, cornflakes and tomato sauce which have fallen out and broken open (or broken) with the motion of the boat.

At the end of the book I have given a comprehensive check list of ship's stores and from this each sea-cook must decide for her (or him) self which items their crew will enjoy and what space they have to use as storage. But don't underestimate the value of the tin in emergencies . . . it can be made into extremely good and satisfying meals with a little ingenuity when necessary. I also include a list of what I consider to be basic necessary utensils, even on a small yacht, for those just starting out on a sailing career.

Scattered through the book you will find tips and hints that I have picked up and found to be useful and reliable. I pass them on in the hope they may prove to be of help to others.

Because many boats now have ovens I have included some recipes using them – each such recipe is clearly indicated.

I have often used convenient items such as tube garlic and bottled lemon juice, dried potatoes and so on in the recipes (because, after all, the book is geared to quick and simply made meals) but if you would rather use the fresh variety then so much the better. I have given weighed amounts in most recipes, specially in ingredients such as butter and flour. However I have given some handy conversion tables (including some for America, Canada and Australia) and differing names for some more common foods.

Except where particularly appropriate I have not given serving suggestions as so much depends on the weather at the time. It is hoped that a quick look through this book before you leave on your trip will show you what meals may be made with the ingredients you have. Alternatively before you set out buy the ingredients necessary to make some of the meals given, checking that the recipes will be easy in heavy seas.

Remember too that it is often helpful to prepare at least one good meal before you leave home bearing in mind that the first long sail of the season is often the most difficult.

Bon appétit!

The Beaufort Scale

The Beaufort Scale is the official wind scale so important to sailors but important to sea-cooks also. Not many amateur sailors deliberately venture forth in a wind force of six on the nose but if you are already at sea and a wind blows up there isn't a lot you can do except plug on and *be ready* in the galley as well as on deck.

No one wants to stand (if standing is indeed possible) juggling items on a galley stove, wiping up spills and feeling more and more queasy, so simplicity (and a bit of forward planning) is essential. Where possible pre-cook if the weather threatens to turn squally, but sometimes in a quick blow-up or a really nasty, and quite often unexpected, sea meals must become 'tin' time. If the weather does threaten to worsen play safe and get out some tins ready to make the meal of your choice. Prepare bits and pieces such as opening and draining tins, or mixing cornflour for sauce, leaving it all safely stowed (in the sink, perhaps) for lunch, dinner or whatever your next meal is. If you have only a few hours left to battle on before making port perhaps it is easiest to keep warm and pleasantly full with bread or toast and mugs of hot, fragrant soup. This is so easy, keeping water hot in a pump action vacuum flask so there is no need to open it to pour; and packets of one-cup soup. The variety of these is endless and can be really satisfying, especially those containing croûtons or meat, as a tide-over. Extra flavouring such as curry or herbs can be added. Occasionally, if the weather is really cold, we add a drop (but just a *drop*) of liquor (whisky or rum) to the cup, to give a lovely warm glow inside. It is *not* recommended to use liquor as a warmer if you are already really cold: warm blankets, a hot water bottle and a cup of hot (and sweet, if you like) tea are much preferable. Personally, I would not use brandy as a warmer either; it is occasionally known to make those feeling sick feel worse.

I have listed each recipe in this book according to the *highest* wind force of the Beaufort scale in which it would be (relatively) easily made. The exceptions are the sections which I feel would not be required in really heavy weather anyway, such as bread and cakes, party nibbles and so on.

However, I do ask you please to remember to adjust for the size of your boat and also for the *direction* of the wind. Force four from aft of the beam can be pleasant, but not so enjoyable when you are thrashing into it on a small boat. What you can prepare on a thirty foot boat is not at all the same as that which you can manage on an eighteen footer under the same wind conditions. The recipes are averaged around boats of about thirty feet.

☆

If you are frying at sea and the wind blows up, use a deep pan such as a pressure cooker; it is safer.

☆

WIND FORCES ONE AND TWO

Light air to light breeze. Sea calm to fairly calm. Possibly has ripples. Wind speed 1-6 knots.

In this wind one can produce virtually any meal, but here are some suggestions.

Mussels, Oyster Style
Barbaree-Grecque Mushrooms
Super Shellfish Soup
Sausage & Bacon with Crispy Potatoes
Salmon & Sweetcorn Pancakes
Light Lunch Salad
Scots Pancakes

WIND FORCE THREE

Gentle breeze. Wind speed 7-10 knots. waves possibly two feet. If you are in a very small boat with a headwind it could be a little choppy.

Chestnut Soup
Pears Coated in Tarragon Mayonnaise
Cheese & Ham Soufflé
Crunchy Herring
Gefilte Fish
Peg's Paella
Prawn Omelette
Chicken in Coconut
Pot Roast in a Pressure Cooker
Rognons Maritimes
Stir-fry Liver & Bacon
Tuna Sauce for Pasta
Bess's Broccoli
Creamy Turnip Mash
Potatoes Anna
Potato Flatties
Vegetable Ideas
Delta Salad
Marion's Salad
Barbara's Biscuits
Janet's Perfect Corn Bread

Mary's Quick Boat Bread
Maureen's Orange or Lemon Biscuits
Never Fail Cake
Plain Scones

WIND FORCE FOUR

Moderate breeze. Wind speed 11-16 knots. Waves possibly three and a half feet. Possibly choppy for any yacht, depending on wind direction and tide.

Cool Mousse
Garlicky Prawns
Baked Potato Ideas
Rough Weather Toad in the Hole
French Toast
Toasted or Fried Sandwiches
Welsh Rarebit
Fellowship Fish Fingers
Fish & Mushrooms
Fish Ideas
Quick Stir-fry Seafood
Barbaree Nasi Goreng (Fried Rice)
Beaut Makan
Boiled Ham
Chinese Chicken with Pineapple
Herby Lamb Kebabs
Gibralter Moussaka
Luncheon Meat with Bacon & Beans
Pork Chops with Mustard
Ros Arcan This & That
Tiddly Kiddly
Tomato Sauce for Spaghetti
Veal Fricassee
Good Old Bubble & Squeak
Ideas for Salads
Ham Pigs
Nutty Fruit Salad
Stuffed Tomato
Jean's Australian Damper

WIND FORCE FIVE

Fresh breeze. Wind speed 17–21 knots. Waves possibly six feet. Could be a nasty wind for any small boat. Not too easy for a moderate sized boat either if you have short seas and are struggling against it.

French Toast (for breakfast)
Scrambled Egg in a Bap
Bread 'n Cheese Lunch
Eggs in a Pan
Eggs with Asparagus
Golden Eye
Mum-in-Law's Mushroom Scramble
Pretend Pizza
The Great Bean Binge
Open Danish Sandwiches
Sealed Sandwiches (Tasty Toasts)
Swiss Sandwiches
Bolognaise Sauce for Pasta
Chilli con Carne
Cooked Ham in Cheese Sauce
Nazeby Left Overs
Please Yourself Pork
Ham with Tomato Sauce

WIND FORCE SIX

Strong breeze, a yachtsman's gale. Wind speed 22–27 knots. Waves possibly nine and a half feet. One rarely chooses to be out in this weather, but when you are caught the following may be useful.

Bacon Sandwiches
Tomato Soup in a Trice
Baked Beans in Pitta Bread
Cheese Burgers
Cheese Nests
Curried Eggs (eggs pre-boiled)
Devilled Sausages or Drumsticks
Potato Cheese Pie
Potato with Cheese and Onion

Pre-made Pancake Fillings
Sosmix
Dutch Uitsmijter
Hamburgers
Sling Together Danwich
Tasty Toasts (when off the wind)
Yvonnës Tuna Curry
Cheoy Lin Mince
Cottage Pie
Ideas for Heavy Weather Meat Meals
Minty Lamb Chops or Herb Chops
Vierge Chicken
Don't overlook the sustaining hot soup
  and bread combination.

WIND FORCES SEVEN, EIGHT AND NINE

Near gale through to strong gale. Wind speeds 28–47 knots. Waves possibly thirteen to twenty-three feet.

Let us hope that yachts and small craft are not caught out in such conditions, but if they are then emergency measures are indicated in the galley. Apart from just preparing and eating what you can to stave off hunger, the following are sometimes possible.

The wind force recommended as normally highest for the preparing of the dishes is in brackets.

David's Force Eight Breakfast
Eggy Muesli (7)
Pick-me-up Vitality Drink (7)
One-cup soups with bread or toast (7-9)
Various soup combinations (7)
Fillings for rolls or pitta bread (9)
Various simple sandwich ideas (6-7)
Beef Chowder (7)
Cheesy Chicken Bake (7)
Force Seven Standbys
Hasty and Hearty (7)
Madras Mince (7)
Ready made sauces (8-9)
Three Bean Salad (7-9)

Basic Recipes and Conversion Tables

CONVERSION TABLES

In the United Kingdom quantities are usually measured using the metric system although some imperial measures are still used (for instance in favourite old recipe books). America still uses cups and spoons of specific quantities while Australia is changing to the metric system. American and United Kingdom solid weights are the same but the liquid quantities are different.

United Kingdom

¼ teaspoon	1.25 ml
½ teaspoon	2.50 ml
1 teaspoon	5 ml
1 tablespoon (1 UK fl. oz)	15 ml
1 teacup (1 UK gill/¼pt)	140 ml
1 10 oz breakfast cup	285 ml
¼ imperial pint	140 ml
½ imperial pint	285 ml
1 imperial pint	570 ml
1¾ imperial pints	1 litre
1 tablespoon flour	½ oz/15g
1 tablespoon fat	oz/15g
1 tablespoon sugar (all level)	½ oz/15g

Australia

¼ teaspoon	1.25 ml
½ teaspoon	2.5 ml
1 teaspoon	5 ml
1 tablespoon	20 ml
¼ cup	62.5 ml
⅓ cup	83 ml
½ cup	125 ml
1 cup	250 ml

United States of America

⅓ cup	3½ UK fl. oz	100 ml
½ cup (1 US gill)	4 UK fl. oz	115 ml
⅔ cup (¼ US pint)	5 UK fl. oz	140 ml
1 cup	8 UK fl. oz	236 ml
1¼ cups (½ US pint)	10 UK fl. oz	285 ml
2 cups (1 US pint)	16 UK fl. oz	425 ml
4 cups (1 US quart)	32 UK fl. oz	1 litre
1 US tablespoon	¾ UK fl. oz	20 ml
1 tablespoon breadcrumbs (heaped)	½ oz	15g
1 tablespoon cornstarch	1oz	25g
1 tablespoon fat	½ oz	15g
1 tablespoon flour	½ oz	15g
1 tablespoon sugar	1 oz	25g
1 tablespoon syrup/treacle	1 oz	25g
1 cup breadcrumbs	4 oz	100g
1 cup brown sugar	6 oz	150g
1 cup confectioner's sugar	4½ oz	105g
1 cup dried fruit	8 oz	225g
1 cup fat	8 oz	225g
1 cup flour	4 oz	100g
1 cup granulated/caster sugar	8 oz	225g
1 cup lentils (or similar)	8 oz	225g
1 cup rice	8 oz	225g
1 cup syrup/honey	12 oz	350g

DIFFERENCES OF NAMES OF
SOME COMMON FOODSTUFFS
(with a few explanations)

British	American
aubergine	eggplant
baking sheet	cookie sheet
baking tin	baking pan
bacon (green)	pork, brined
bacon (smoked)	pork, brined then smoked
base grilling (barbecue type)	grill
beans, baked	baked beans *in tomato sauce*
beans, broad	lima beans
beans, French	haricots verts
beans, haricot	navy beans
beans, runner	snap beans (nearest equivalent, they are bigger than French beans but smaller than runner beans)
beetroot	beet
bicarbonate of soda	baking soda
biscuits, cheese type	crackers
biscuits, soda type	saltines, soda crackers
biscuits, sweet	cookies
blood heat	luke warm
bottling	canning
butter, unsalted	sweet butter (nearest equivalent)
butter, 4 oz	1 stick
celeriac	celery root or celeri-rave

chicory/endive–In Britain we call endive what the French call chicory, and vice versa

chicory (is much like. . .)	Witloof chicory (French or Italian endive)
endive (is much like. . .)	escarole or chicory escarole (Batavian endive)

British	American
chilli powder	US chilli powder is blended with other spices. The UK variety is pure and much hotter. In US substitute cayenne for UK chilli powder. The US cayenne is much hotter than the British.
chocolate, plain	bitter chocolate
cornflour	cornstarch
courgette	zucchini
cream, single	half and half (usually used for coffee in USA. It is thinner than British single cream)
cream, whipping	light whipping cream
cream, double	heavy cream
curd cheese	pot or farmers' cheese
dessicated coconut	unsweetened shredded coconut
essence	extract
flour, plain	all-purpose flour
flour, strong	bread flour
frying pan	skillet
gammon	bacon from hind quarter, cured while still attached to body
glacé	candied
grill (top heat)	broil
gut	clean
ham	bacon from hind quarter, brined or dry cured, on its own
jams (with fruit)	preserves (with fruit)
jellies (without fruit)	jellies (without fruit)
jelly	jello, gelatin dessert
marrow (is like. . .)	a huge, overgrown zucchini

British	American
mince (raw)	ground beef, hamburger beef
oatmeal, pinhead	Irish oatmeal
oats, porridge	rolled oats
rasher	slice
sieve	sift
spring onion	green onion, scallion on East coast
shrimps or prawns	shrimp
stewing steak	braising beef
sugar, caster	granulated (caster is finer; grind a little time in electric blender)
sugar, icing	confectioners' sugar (a little different in USA in that it has some cornstarch mixed into it)
sultanas	golden raisins
swede	rutabaga

EXPLANATIONS

Eggs are of large (2 oz/50g) size unless otherwise stated.

Spoon and cup measurements are level unless otherwise stated.

Tinned products The weight of the contents varies from manufacturer to manufacturer so I have given approximate sizes. A little difference will not matter.

Gelatine Generally, use ½ – 1 oz/15 – 25g gelatine to set 1 imperial pint/570 ml using less in cool weather, more in hot and more for acidic liquids or liquids containing a good proportion of solid material (e.g. fruit, meat).

American gelatin 1 US tablespoon can solidify 2 US cups (1 US pint) of liquid.

Yeast 1 packet in UK gives a scant tablespoon (0.25 oz/7g) which will rise 1½ lb/750g of strong flour. (This information was taken from McDougall's Country Life Dried Yeast – a 'fast action' yeast, no need to prove before adding to bread and ideal for use afloat). In USA a packet of yeast will rise about 6½ cups of all-purpose flour.

My American friend tells me it is not really satisfactory to try to substitute corn syrup and molasses for golden syrup and treacle.

BASIC RECIPES

Most sailing wives will already have their favourite basic recipes for such things as short crust pastry, but for those who normally do not take on the task of catering and cooking the occasion could arise when you are forced to do so, perhaps because your 'Girl Friday' is seasick, or has left the boat and you have not yet found a replacement.

Perhaps you *can* cook but have temporarily forgotten the precise ingredients for Yorkshire pudding.

Whatever the reason you may be seeking these simple facts I have included this short section to help you.

In the pastry recipes you may notice a slight variation in the conversion from imperial to metric measurements. This is to make the more precise adjustment necessary to give the proper balance to the ingredients for good pastry.

Cooking rice (Chinese Method) This takes away the need for large amounts of water or of draining. If cooked in a deep non-stick pan there is no mess (and little waste).

For each person you will require 2 oz/50g long grain rice (or Basmati, 'easy cook' etc.) This must be washed very well in several changes of water (salt water is perfectly all right as long as you wash out the salt with fresh water in the last washing). The water should run clear showing that all the coating of starch has been washed off otherwise it will stick. Even 'easy cook' rice benefits from a wash. This may be done in the pan in which you will cook the rice.

Drain well then put into pot again. Pour in water to cover the rice by about a ½ inch (1¼cm). This is about 14 oz/400g rice to 1 pint/570 fl.oz water but if making a large quantity of rice decrease the water quantity slightly. Add a little salt.

Cook quickly till the water boils, then turn heat down as low as possible and cook, covered tightly, for a further 5 minutes or so until the rice looks fairly dry. Turn heat off and leave rice covered for about 15 minutes. You should have separate fluffy grains. Fork up and leave till required, covered. The rice (if still damp) can be dried again for a short while in an oven but it should not be necessary. Do *not* use short grain rice. A knob of butter added to the water before boiling will help keep the grains separate.

Pasta dishes are a useful stand-by. Generally 1 oz/25g pasta makes about 3 oz/75g cooked, but use as much as you know your crew will manage. (Average helping = 2 oz/50g per person.) Use instructions on box if possible as pasta does vary in its cooking times, but as a rough guide it should be dropped into a large pot of rapidly boiling salted water.

Small pasta such as vermicelli should be ready in about 4–5 minutes while macaroni and spaghetti will take longer, say 10–12 minutes. Test by biting a small piece. It should be 'al dente' – that is tender yet strong enough to bite in two cleanly. Add a little oil to the water to prevent sticking and stir occasionally during cooking. Drain well.

Lasagne is a little different. It is best to cook a few pieces at a time. Care should be taken not to break the leaves and when stirring do so gently, lifting and turning. It will take about 12 minutes to cook but test as above on a small corner. Lift out carefully and drop into a basin of cold water, then lift out one by one and pat dry. Keep separate until using.

Most pasta can be pre-cooked then gently reheated in a little water, but it is best eaten freshly cooked when possible, resorting to a quick reheat only in emergencies.

I would not try to reheat lasagne but of course if you make up a dish of mince, cheese sauce, with leaves of lasagne in it, then reheating in an oven is quite easy.

> ☆
> *To convert plain flour to self-raising flour add 1 level teaspoon baking powder to each 2 oz/50g plain flour and mix in well.*
> ☆

Pastry making I list below only the most common pastry types. It is not something you will wish to make in bad weather as it takes time and a flat surface, but it *is* nice to know how so you can conjure up surprises such as a fruit pie or some chocolate choux buns, so here goes:

SUET PASTRY

Use self-raising flour for this pastry or add baking powder to plain flour as explained above if you have no self-raising flour to hand.

Preparation & cooking time: approx. 3½ hours

8 oz/210g self-raising flour
½ level teaspoon salt
4 oz/105g pre-packed shredded suet (or grated butcher's suet)
5fl.oz/150ml water
dash of freshly ground pepper

1. Sift flour and add salt, pepper and shredded suet. Rub together lightly.
2. Add enough cold water gradually to make a softish dough, but not too soft to work.
3. Roll out on floured board as for short crust pastry, using short light strokes.

Use to line bowls for steamed meat or fruit puddings by cutting out a segment of a third of the circle. Place the large piece of pastry in a greased bowl and ease to fit. Press join to seal. Fill with a mixture of, for example, tinned stew (if the stew is very sloppy take out some gravy). Use the remaining pastry to make a lid. Press on gently at edges to seal. Cover the bowl with *two* layers of buttered greaseproof paper with a fold across the centre to allow for expansion. Tie firmly and tightly with string, making a loop across the top with an extra piece so the pudding can be lifted easily when hot.

The puddings are steamed in a large pan of boiling water. Steam a 1 lb/½ kg basin of pudding for about three hours, being careful not to let it go off the boil or to boil dry. Because of the long cooking the gravy (or water if using fresh meat) should be about a half to three quarters of the way up the basin. These meat puddings are best well seasoned and with a good sprinkling of herbs of your choice. A little mixed mustard stirred in before cooking is also tasty.

You may also make a fruit pudding in the same way.

If you have a pressure cooker follow the instructions for that when cooking the pudding. A pressure cooker saves about two thirds of the time taken for normal cooking, well worth while on a boat if you have room to store one.

SHORT CRUST PASTRY

Use as little water as possible to mix to a malleable dough and use cold water and keep everything as cool as you can. Do not overmix.

Rest the made pastry when possible, wrapped in polythene film, for half an hour before using. This helps to stop it shrinking during cooking.

Oven necessary
Preparation & cooking time: 40 minutes plus ½ hour rest

6 oz/200g plain flour
3 oz/100g margarine (cut into small cubes)
pinch salt
very cold water to mix

1. Sift flour and salt.
2. Using tips of fingers rub fat into flour till like breadcrumbs. Try to keep fingers cool – dip in cold water and dry if necessary.
3. Add a little water – begin with 1 tablespoon. Mix with a knife. Add more water as necessary – enough to bind to a stiff dough. Add more water later rather than earlier.
4. Use fingers to squeeze gently into a ball.
5. Wrap up in polythene and leave to rest or until ready to use.

If you need a rich sweet pastry add ½ oz/15g more butter (it is better to use butter than margarine), 2 tablespoons sugar, 1 egg yolk and less water than above. Mix the egg yolk with a tablespoon water before adding.

When rolling out the pastry use a lightly floured board or table top. Roll with short strokes away from you, and turn the pastry a quarter turn frequently until size is correct. A light touch keeps the pastry light. Use as required.

Generally this pastry cooks in a fairly hot oven, 425°F/220°C/Gas Mark 7) for about 25–30 minutes. It should be a golden brown. Dust with sugar after cooling if desired.

If you are using fruit for a filling cut a vent in the pastry to allow steam to escape and don't use more than a tablespoon or two of liquid if using tinned fruit. Fill the pie well with fruit, mounding the centre.

ROUGH PUFF PASTRY

Oven necessary
Preparation & cooking time: about 10 minutes to prepare then 15–25 minutes depending on thickness – should be golden.

The easiest rough puff pastry I know is the one given by John Tovey in his book, *Entertaining with Tovey*, which he has kindly allowed me to use here.

1lb/450g strong plain flour
generous pinch salt
½lb/225g soft American lard or shortening
1 tablespoon lemon juice made up to
    ½ pt/300 ml with very cold water

1. Sieve the flour into a bowl and break up the fats into ½ oz/15g pieces and dot them about over the flour. Coat by shaking gently.
2. Gently make a well in the centre and into it pour the very cold water and lemon juice. Mix with a knife, cutting across and across till the lumps are very small.
3. Lightly flour a board and turn out the mixture, scraping out all the pieces. Shape gently into the shape of a brick with the short end of the brick nearest you and the long sides running down from your left to your right side.
4. Hold the rolling pin at each end, never in the middle and treat it with delicacy. Just tap the merest outline of the rolling pin in the middle, top and bottom of the 'brick' and then, starting at the impression immediately in front of you, just lightly – oh so lightly – give the rolling pin a good gentle push and remove your hands. Never bring the rolling pin back towards you with any pressure. Always make sharp, soft movements away from you, slowly but surely stretching the pastry out into a shape roughly measuring 16 × 5 in (40 × 12 cm).
5. Picture this long rectangle in three equal parts and fold the piece facing you up and over the middle third and bring the top third down on top of these two thirds. You want this pastry to be as light as possible, so trap the air at this stage by gently tapping down on the three open layers at the short ends at your left and right. Give this piece of dough a quarter turn – imagine your dough is the hour hand pointing to 6 o'clock, and turn it to 9 o'clock. Leave it aside for two or three minutes.
6. Repeat this process three more times, flouring your work area well between each rolling so the dough does not stick. You may find when you turn the bottom third of dough up over the middle third there is a surplus of flour. Brush this off with a brush (a clean, new 6 in (15 cm) paint brush is good for this). With each rolling, the texture becomes smoother and on the fourth and last rolling, the dough is even slightly resistant, so don't force it in any way. Sometimes it just will not roll to the above measurements so, whatever you do, don't force it to this size at the expense of knocking the air out.
7. Pop the dough into a polythene bag and leave to chill if possible.

Use this dough for vol-au-vents, steak and kidney pie and so on. Cook in a hot oven – 450°F/230°C/Gas Mark 8 – till well risen and golden. Roll out to approximately ⅛ in/3 cm thickness, still working lightly. Cut out the shapes and place on a slightly dampened metal tray, then chill again if possible. When ready to cook, place a well buttered piece of greaseproof paper on top (greased side down on to the pastry). Prick through the paper and pastry with

☆

If you wish to pre-cook meat, store it in foil, then it can be re-heated in the foil in the oven or under a moderate grill. It will have to be turned several times under the grill to ensure even heating.

☆

a sharp pointed knife (about 6 pricks to a 3½ in/9 cm vol-au-vent). Check after about 12 minutes' cooking. Pre-cook meat if making steak and kidney pie.

CHOUX PASTRY

Oven necessary
Preparation time: approximately 20 minutes

Measure the ingredients for this as exactly as you can as it is easily spoiled.

> *4 oz/110g plain flour*
> *4 oz/110g butter*
> *2 oz/50g sugar*
> *2 eggs (large)*
> *10 fl.oz/285 ml water*
> *pinch salt*

1. Put butter, water, salt and sugar into a pan.
2. Bring to boil slowly. Butter and sugar must be melted before the water boils.
3. Have sieved flour *ready* and as soon as the water boils remove from heat and tip in the flour quickly. Beat well.
4. As soon as the mixture leaves the side of the pan and forms a ball stop beating and leave to cool.
5. Beat eggs and incorporate with the mixture slowly. The mixture should be of a dropping consistency. That is, it drops in *thick* blobs from a spoon fairly easily. Do not add more egg when this consistency is reached.

☆
Remove soft fat from the tops of soups or stews etc. by laying a piece of kitchen paper on top them removing gently. Repeat till all fat has been absorbed.
☆

CHOCOLATE CHOUX BUNS

Cooking time: 25 minutes then time to cool and fill

Wet a baking tray and drop a tablespoonful of the pastry at a time onto the tray. Cook in a hot oven (400°F/200°C/Gas Mark 6) for about 25 minutes. The buns should be pale brown, crisp and hollow.

Make a hole in the side of each with a skewer to allow steam to escape, then cool. Fill with whipped cream or confectioner's custard and top with melted chocolate. Eat the same day.

DUMPLINGS FOR STEWS

Preparation time: 10 minutes then cook with stews. These add bulk to a pot of stew and are flavoursome as well.

> *8 oz/225g plain flour*
> *3 level teaspoons baking powder*
> *large pinch salt*
> *1 oz/25g butter*
> *5fl.oz/140 ml milk*
> *1 beaten egg*
> *½ teaspoon curry powder*

1. Melt butter. Sift flour, baking powder and salt together.
2. Add egg to sifted flour mixture with melted butter and add milk slowly to make a stiff but workable batter (i.e. not crumbly)
3. About quarter of an hour before stew is ready, drop dessertspoonfuls of the mixture into the pan, cover and allow to simmer for about a quarter of an hour. The dumplings should be puffed up and fluffy.

YORKSHIRE PUDDING BATTER

Oven necessary
Serves 4
Preparation & cooking time: 45 minutes plus
1 hour standing time

4 oz/100g plain flour
2 eggs
3 tablespoons oil or dripping
½ pt/285ml milk
large pinch salt

1. Sift flour and salt.
2. Beat eggs and add to flour. Beat well.
3. Add enough milk to make a thick runny batter. (I find half a pint is just about right.)
4. Beat well. Stand for at least 1 hour.
5. Before using beat well again.
6. While 'standing' the batter place two thirds of the fat into an oven dish or tin (about 6in × 8in – 15cm × 20cm) and heat in hot oven (400°F/200°C/Gas Mark 6–7) till it sizzles.
7. Add the remainder of the oil to the batter and beat briefly. Pour the batter into the hot fat and cook for about 30–35 minutes in the oven until risen and golden round the edges. The centre will probably be flatter and creamy.

BASIC PANCAKE BATTER

(To fill when required)
Preparation & cooking time: 30 minutes

5 oz/125g plain flour
large pinch salt
2 eggs
1 tablespoon oil
milk to mix

1. Sift flour and salt.
2. Make a well in centre and add eggs and oil. Beat well.
3. Add milk gradually until the mixture is like thick cream, stirring. This usually takes a little less than half a pint (285ml). Beat till smooth.
4. Allow to stand for at least half an hour. If you can make the batter early and leave it for a couple of hours it will be even better.
5. Beat again then pour from a jug slowly into a hot, lightly greased pan – a frying pan, omelette pan, or griddle if you have one. Use just enough batter to coat the base of the pan, or (if using a griddle) make a circle about six in. (15cm) diameter.
6. Cook over a medium flame for a minute then flip over with a spatula or knife and cook other side.
7. When golden on both sides transfer to a folded tea towel or a plate. Between each lay a strip of greaseproof paper to keep the pancakes separate. They may be kept wrapped in a damp towel for 2 days.

BASIC PLAIN OMELETTE

Preparation & cooking time: 10 minutes

This quantity is enough for an omelette for one made in a fairly small frying pan. Do *not* use milk to mix as this will make the omelette tough.

3 small eggs
1 tablespoon cold water
seasoning to taste

1. Beat the eggs and water together with the seasoning briefly. Do not overbeat.
2. Grease a frying pan with just enough butter to swirl round the base and sides. Heat gently until it sizzles.
3. Pour in the omelette mixture and stir gently once or twice with a fork to allow top to be cooked, and lift round the edges occasionally.
4. When the base is golden and the top is still creamy soft tilt the pan and fold the omelette in half. Slide onto a hot plate.

All sorts of fillings (savoury, herby or sweet) may be added before the end of cooking.

22

BAKED CUSTARD

Oven necessary
Serves 4
Preparation & cooking time: 1 hour

3/4 pt/425 ml milk
2 oz/50g sugar
3 medium eggs
1/2 teaspoon vanilla essence
large pinch salt

1. Heat oven to 325°F/170°C/Gas Mark 3.
2. Prepare a large baking pan half full of hot water and place in oven. Have ready a dish large enough to contain the milk mixture and which will fit inside the pan of water.
3. Scald the milk in a saucepan.
4. Mix eggs together lightly and add to milk, stirring. Do not beat.
5. Add sugar and salt and stir in gently.
6. Add a drop or two of essence if required.
7. Strain the milk and egg mixture into the prepared dish, put dish into pan and bake until firm. Test by pushing a knife blade into the custard; it should come out clean. There will be a skin in the custard. Cooking time is approximately 40 minutes.

To scald milk Heat gently until bubbles show around the edge of the pan, then take off heat. Do not boil.

BASIC RICE PUDDING

Oven necessary
Serves 4
Preparation & cooking time: 4 hours

2 oz/50g short grain rice
1 pt/570 ml milk
2 oz/50g sugar
2 tablespoons cream (optional)
4 drops vanilla essence
knob of butter (optional)

1. Heat oven to 325°F/170°C/Gas Mark 3.
2. Take a little butter and grease an oven-proof dish.
3. Combine the rice, milk, sugar, essence and cream if using. A knob of butter may be added for extra creaminess. Pour into the prepared dish.
4. Bake for about 3½ hours. The pudding should have a creamy consistency and a pale nut-brown skin.

For a good substitute for a boat see Rice Pudding in a Vacuum Flask in The Sweet Course chapter.

GROUND RICE OR SEMOLINA

Serves 4
Preparation & cooking time: 10 minutes and then cooling time

There should be instructions for making the above on their boxes or packets but if you have removed them to storage jars and cannot remember how to make them the following is a good rough guide:

For each pint/570 ml milk mix together
1 oz/25g sugar (2 dessertspoons)
2 oz/50g ground rice or semolina (6 slightly
*   heaped dessertspoons)*

1. Reserve a little of the milk to mix with the dry ingredients, making a smooth paste.
2. Heat the rest of the milk in a saucepan.
3. Stir in the paste gently when the milk is warm, and bring slowly to the boil. Turn heat very low and stir till the mixture thickens.
4. Pour into a dish to cool. The mixture will thicken more as it cools, so if very thick in the pan add a little more milk.

A knob of butter improves the flavour and you may add essences or flavouring to taste.

Serve on its own, or with fruit; with jam on top, or honey.

Night Passages and Breakfasts

The vacuum flask with pump-action lid from which you can, in the night, help yourself to an instant hot drink without fear of spills or of waking the off-duty crew by rattling kettles, is a godsend. Rather than put soup into the pump flask where it may clog, and in any case restricts the watch to one variety, I fill the flask with boiling water which can then be mixed with a one-cup soup, meat or yeast extract, drinking chocolate or other proprietary preparations, whenever it is required by the crew on watch. Hot chocolate with a dash of mixed spice in it is good, and, if it is really cold, a small drop (no more than a dessertspoon) of rum, whisky or brandy added warms you up wonderfully.

On an average, uneventful night sail we find watches are made very pleasant if a bar of dark chocolate is left handy. We find a three-hour watch is about right in reasonable weather, less in heavy, but of course everyone has to find their own level on this point. Before we turn in we make ourselves a hot drink from the flask – usually soup of some sort.

Breakfast After a night sail breakfast can be one of the best meals of the day. You really feel you have earned it. Unless you are spending the day in port or at anchor it is also a fairly important meal on board a small craft. You are never quite sure when your next meal will be, and if you have already been at sea for a night then you are more than ready for breakfast. We tend to have a bowl of cereal early in the morning when it is light and there is a watch change, and have a proper breakfast later when the crew have all had some sleep and are awake again.

Breakfast starters Choose from your favourite cereal, muesli, instant porridge, hot baby cereal, or fruit juice. Buy your fruit juice in the oblong cartons for easy storage. When open stow with the cut corner nipped tight with a bulldog clip; it then keeps about two or three days at room temperature. Another idea is dried fruit which can be soaked overnight in a watertight container when required (or eaten dry if you like it). For emergencies have on hand some grated cheese or hard boiled eggs.

If one of your crew feels queasy then stick to cereal which stays down well, and is sustaining.

The following ideas may be helpful for bad weather breakfasts.

Cracked eggs may be boiled safely if first wrapped tightly in foil.

SCRAMBLED EGG IN A BAP

Serves 1   Wind force: 5
Preparation & cooking time: 10 minutes

*1 bap
2 eggs
1 tablespoon milk
1 oz/25g sharp cheese
seasoning to taste*

24

1. Grate the cheese with a potato peeler.
2. In a non-stick pan (if possible) scramble eggs, milk and seasoning by mixing together well and cooking slowly until just set but meanwhile adding cheese slowly.
3. Continue to cook slowly, allowing cheese to melt.
4. As soon as eggs start to set remove from heat and spoon over base of bap. Place lid of bap on top and serve at once.

FRENCH TOAST

Serves 1   Wind force: 5
Preparation & cooking time: 5 minutes

1 egg
1 slice bread
seasoning to taste
oil to lightly grease a pan

1. In deep dish break egg up with fork.
2. Add seasoning and whip lightly.
3. Dip both sides of bread (thin slices are best) into egg, soaking liberally.
4. Heat frying pan and fry bread quickly, pouring in the extra egg as you turn the bread over to fry the other side.

A touch of mustard or dried herb may be added before cooking. When cooked, cinnamon and sugar, syrup, jam or honey may be added.

BACON SANDWICH

Serves 1   Wind force: 6
Preparation & cooking time: 5 minutes

1. Toast two slices of bread and leave in grill pan.
2. Dry fry bacon or ham rashers and place between the toast slices using bacon fat, if enough, to butter the toast. A lightly whipped egg may be fried and added if weather permits.

EGGY MUESLI

Serves 1   Wind force: 7
Preparation time: 5 minutes

3 tablespoons muesli
5 fl. oz/140 ml milk or natural yoghurt
1 beaten egg
sugar to taste if necessary

Mix well together and eat at once.

PICK-ME-UP VITALITY DRINK

Serves 1   Wind force: 7
Preparation time: 1 minute

1. Beat one raw egg and a teaspoonful of honey into a cup (8 fl. oz/225 ml) of fruit juice of your choice.
2. Pour out and drink.
   If the weather is awful then mix the above in a screw top jar, shaking well.

DAVID'S FORCE EIGHT BREAKFAST

Serves 1 (each to his own)   Wind force: 8
Preparation time: 5 minutes

bacon and egg as required

1. Cut bacon into small pieces with scissors.
2. Drop into deep pan.
3. Fry till soft, shaking occasionally.
4. Add egg(s) to taste.
5. When cooked slide onto slice of bread, top with second slice and eat.

☆
Grease pans with oil. Butter, unless unsalted, can cause sticking.
☆

Soups and Starters

SOUPS

Soup in a mug to warm you inside and out when on watch, or to keep you going in bad weather is indispensable, but unless some planning is done, it is hazardous to try to produce a really good sustaining soup if you are bucketing about in strong winds using pans full of liquid.

I set great store in having a good big vacuum flask which can be filled before I leave, and in being ready for emergencies with the back-up of one-cup soups for snacks, night sailing and emergencies. Nourishing soups plus bread or rolls make a satisfying meal if you are caught in a gale, specially if you have enough to serve some every two or three hours. If you don't need it all on the way you can always serve the left-overs for a snack on arrival to keep the crew happy till dinner is ready.

One thing to remember . . . tomatoes have been known to make those inclined to sea-sickness feel very queasy in rough weather.

☆

If you have an oven, put stale bread or rolls into a wet paper bag and bake for 5-15 minutes in a moderate oven, depending on size. This will freshen them up.

☆

GAZPACHO

Serves 4   Wind force: in port
Preparation time: 30 minutes

This dish is lovely on a summer evening.

2 slices bread
½ cucumber
1 lb/450g tomatoes
1 tablespoon pimiento (optional)
1 large green pepper
1 squeeze garlic (or one clove)
1 small onion
1 tablespoon vinegar
3 tablespoons olive oil
seasoning to taste
½ pt/285 ml water

1. Crumble bread and soak in some water till pasty, squeezing it to help it along, then drain well.
2. Chop finely the tomato, cucumber, pepper, pimiento and onion.
3. Add olive oil, vinegar and water.
4. Mix well and add crushed garlic.
5. Add bread, stirring to mix again. Season well to taste.

Serve cold with little dishes of extra tomato, cucumber, onion and pepper, all finely chopped, and some extra diced bread for sprinkling on top.

If possible, a small rotary grater is handy to have on board for this type of dish; it saves all the dicing.

Prawns, langoustines and other shellfish may seem expensive but for a treat they are incomparable. Do not overlook the fact that a wonderful soup may be made from the heads, tails and shells. The following is one we developed as we went along and is very tasty:

SUPER SHELLFISH SOUP

Serves 4   Wind force: 2
Preparation & cooking time: 15 minutes

remains of prawns, langoustines, crabs or
   other shellfish
any liquid in which they were cooked
¾ pint/½ l water (including cooking liquid)
1 tin (10.4 oz/295g) condensed cream of celery
   soup
1 tablespoon tomato purée
approximately 2 oz/50g grated cheese
seasoning to taste

1. Place all the remains from the shellfish into a large pan, adding any liquid you have from the initial preparation of the fish.
2. Make up to ¾ pint (½ litre) with the water and boil for about 10 minutes then strain well.
3. Return liquid to the pan, discarding the fish, add all the ingredients except the seasoning and heat thoroughly.
4. Taste and adjust seasoning and serve hot with crusty bread.

TOMATO IN A TRICE

Serves 4   Wind force: 6
Preparation & cooking time: 5 minutes

2 × 14 oz/400g tins tomatoes and the juice
1 dessertspoon lemon juice
1 tablespoon sugar
1 tablespoon Worcester sauce
5 oz/140g carton yoghurt
seasoning to taste

1. Place all ingredients except seasoning and yoghurt in deep pan. Bring to boil slowly, breaking up tomatoes as you stir.
2. Add yoghurt and season to taste.
3. Pour into mugs and drink at once.
   This may be served cold if desired.
   Remember the tip about tomatoes possibly making one feel queasy in a nasty sea.

IDEAS FOR SOUPS

Preparation & cooking time: Wind force 7
10 minutes approximately

Try some of the following different combinations, completing with milk as advised on tins and adding different herbs, spices etc. to suit yourself.

- Condensed tomato and vegetable
- Condensed pea and consommé
- Condensed celery and vegetable
- Condensed chicken and mushroom or celery
- Condensed tomato and celery

Other ingredients which could be added are:

- Shrimps or prawns
- Bottled oysters or mussels
- Small tin of chicken breasts, chopped up

- Sherry
- Cream
- Small tin of tuna, drained
- Left over mashed potato
- Small tin of sweetcorn
- Dried onions or peppers or mixed vegetables
- Small tin of ham, chopped up

A little curry powder added to any of the above makes an interesting flavour. The above are all satisfying served with bread or rolls, previously buttered. Suit the combination to the weather.

STARTERS

Generally, when at sea, we don't bother serving starters but in port they make a good meal super. Perhaps someone less lazy than I would like to make them at sea. They are easy enough in fairly calm weather, except the Crumby Garlic Mushrooms, which are much better done when stable.

CRUMBY GARLIC MUSHROOMS

Serves 4   Wind force: in port
Preparation & cooking time: 10 minutes

1lb/450g button mushrooms
2 tablespoons plain flour
1 egg
1 tablespoon water
4 oz/100g breadcrumbs
4 oz/100g sharp cheese
large squeeze garlic purée (2 cloves, crushed)
seasoning to taste
oil to fry

1. Wipe mushrooms, remove long stalks and use elsewhere. Coat mushroom caps in flour.

2. Grate cheese and mix with breadcrumbs.
3. Whisk egg and water together and dip mushrooms into the mixture then into the breadcrumb mixture.
4. Pour a fair amount of oil into deep frying pan and stir in garlic.
5. When really hot, cook mushrooms quickly, turning till crisp. Do these in batches, drain on kitchen paper and keep hot. Serve when all are ready.
   A little tartare sauce is good for dipping.

BARBAREE-GRECQUE MUSHROOMS

Serves 4   Wind force: 2
Preparation time: 10 minutes plus half an hour marinade

2 × 7½ oz/190g tins button mushrooms, well
*   drained or 1lb/450g fresh mushrooms*
1 tomato
2 tablespoons french dressing
2 tablespoons white wine
½ teaspoon dried tarragon
½ teaspoon thyme
generous squeeze garlic purée or 2 crushed
*   cloves*

1. Skin and chop the tomato finely.
2. Shake the french dressing in a bottle, or mix well, and pour out two tablespoons into a bowl.
3. Add herbs, garlic and tomato and stir well together.
4. Add wine and mix in.

☆

Hold tomatoes over gas flame on a fork for a few seconds. This makes them easy to peel. So does plunging them into boiling water for a few seconds.

☆

28

5. Add mushrooms and mix in well.
6. Leave to stand at least half an hour, to marinade.
Serve with french bread.

MUSSELS, OYSTER STYLE

Serves 4   Wind force: 2
Preparation & cooking time: 10 minutes

> *4 pts mussels in shells (approx. 48 mussels –*
> * allow for some waste)*
> *1 small onion*
> *1 pt/570 ml water*
> *1 pt/570 ml white wine*

1. Peel and chop onion finely. Clean and scrape mussels, discarding any which remain open or float in a bowl of water.
2. Place water, wine and onion in deep pan and bring to boil.
3. Tip in mussels, a few at a time, ensuring they are covered, and cook with the lid on for only 20 seconds, till shells have opened. Drain and cool.
   Serve in half shells like oysters with Tabasco sauce, lemon wedges and brown bread and butter.
   Do not overcook – they should literally just have time to open and be almost raw. Discard any which remain closed.

PRAWNS IN AVOCADO
(from *Tasty Dishes with Norwegian Prawns*)

Serves 4   Wind force: 3
Preparation time: 10 minutes

> *2 avocado pears*
> *5 oz/125g clean, peeled prawns*
> *3 tablespoons mayonnaise*
> *3 tablespoons sour cream (use drop of lemon*
> * juice to sour)*
> *more lemon juice to taste*
> *dill seeds to garnish*

1. Cut the avocados in half lengthways, remove stones and brush edges with lemon juice.
2. Mix prawns, mayonnaise and sour cream, adding a little more lemon juice to taste. Pile into the avocado halves.
   Garnish with dill seeds and serve.

CHESTNUT SOUP

Serves 4   Wind force 3
Preparation & cooking time: 40 minutes

> *small tin unsweetened chestnut purée*
> *2 oz/50g unsalted butter*
> *small onion, chopped*
> *2 pt/1 lt chicken stock (fresh or made with a cube)*
> *small carrot, finely chopped*
> *seasoning*
> *half-pint/295 ml whipping cream*

1. Melt butter gently. Add onion and cook until soft, stirring.
2. Add stock, chestnut purée, carrot and seasoning.
3. Simmer for 30 minutes. Cool a little.
4. Push through a sieve, or blend if you have a blender.
5. Return to pan and add cream. Heat gently, stirring.
   Serve with Melba toast or crispbreads.

PEARS COATED IN TARRAGON MAYONNAISE

Serves 4   Wind force:3
Preparation time: 10 minutes

1/4 pt/140 ml thick mayonnaise
2 teaspoons tarragon vinegar
4 tablespoons cream
2 teaspoons dried tarragon
salt
1 lemon and few lettuce leaves to garnish
chilli powder
2 fat ripe pears

1. Mix together the mayonnaise, cream and vinegar.
2. Stir in the tarragon and mix well.
3. Add salt and pinch chilli powder to taste. Set aside.
4. Cut pears in half, cut out centres and peel.
5. Lay hollow side down on a lettuce leaf, then spoon over the tarragon mayonnaise.
6. Garnish with a lemon twist on top.
    The centres of avocado pears may also be filled with the above mayonnaise.

GARLICY PRAWNS

Serves 4   Wind force: 4
Preparation & cooking time: 5 minutes

1/2 oz/15g butter
squeeze of garlic purée (1 clove, crushed)
2 tablespoons oil
2 tablespoons chopped fresh parsley
12 oz/350g peeled prawns
2 teaspoons lemon juice

1. Heat butter and oil and add garlic. Fry for 2 minutes.
2. Add prawns and cook quickly for 1 minute (if using raw prawns cook 2 minutes).
3. Toss round the pan with a spoon to cook evenly.
4. Stir in parsley and lemon juice and serve at once with brown bread and butter.

COOL MOUSSE

Serves 4   Wind force: 4
Preparation time: 15 minutes

1/2 lb/225g full fat cream cheese
1/2 cucumber
2 tablespoons lemon juice
small pinch cayenne pepper
seasoning to taste
lettuce
crispbreads, biscuits

1. Skin, grate and drain cucumber. Cream cheese till very soft.
2. Stir in cucumber, add lemon juice and cayenne pepper. Season. If possible leave in a cool place for a while.
    Serve on a bed of lettuce, with crispbreads or biscuits.

☆
Add a few grains of rice to your lettuce container, to keep the lettuce crisper.
☆

Lunches, Snacks or Suppers

The following recipes are all interchangeable according to the wind and your mood.

I feel snack meals are a vitally important part of cooking on small boats, particularly in rough weather. They are the answer if the sea-cook cannot cope with a full scale meal and they may be eaten at any time. They can be easily put together and will warm and fill the crew.

However, it is also important that the snack should be appetising and, if possible, 'different'. From bitter experience I have learned how dull a ham sandwich or baked beans on toast can be. But when you have a few ideas in hand meals can be made much more pleasant with very little effort.

Planning is again important: croûtons and grated cheese can be prepared in advance and kept quite a time in screw top jars as can crisply fried and crumbled bacon pieces, and *dry* breadcrumbs. All make interesting toppings to otherwise dull dishes.

SAUSAGE AND BACON WITH CRISPY POTATOES

Serves as many   Wind force: 2 or in harbour
as you wish
Preparation & cooking time: 20 minutes

potatoes
margarine or butter
porridge oats
sausages
bacon
seasoning to taste

1. Boil enough potatoes, of reasonably even size, for the crew.
2. Toss in melted butter or margarine and coat with porridge oats. Keep hot, tossing now and then till brown and crisp.
3. Meanwhile, fry sausages and bacon (and an egg, if you wish).
   Serve with the potatoes, adding mushrooms or other ingredients if you wish – a very amenable dish.

CHEESE & HAM SOUFFLE

Serves 4   Wind force 3
Preparation and cooking time: approx. 40 minutes

1 x 10 oz/295g tin condensed ham & cheese soup
   with wine
2 oz/50g Cheddar cheese, grated
2 fl.oz/50 ml milk
4 medium eggs, separated, plus 1 extra egg white
large pinch cayenne pepper

1. Mix together the soup, cheese, milk and cayenne pepper.
2. Add the egg yolks.
3. Whisk whites separately in a clean bowl until stiff.
4. Gently fold whites into soup mixture. Pour into a lightly-greased 2.5 pt dish (soufflé if possible).
5. Sprinkle over more grated cheese if desired.
6. Bake in a moderate oven (350°F/180°C/Gas Mark 4) for 30-35 minutes until well risen and golden.
   Serve immediately, with salad.

Keep a few tins of assorted toast toppers in your stores cupboard. These are quite tasty on their own, but if you add a few extra ingredients they can become quick, satisfying and interesting snacks. Try chopped spring onions, coriander powder, cumin powder, deseeded and chopped tomatoes, curry powder or grated cheese.

ROUGH WEATHER TOAD IN THE HOLE

Oven necessary
Serves 4   Wind force: 4
Preparation & cooking time: 40 minutes

Make batter 1 hour beforehand if possible and leave to stand. If the weather is bad make the batter in a large jar with a lid screwed firmly on – breaking egg up first in jar with a fork. This allows you to shake it well with no fear of spilling.

1 lb/450g pork sausages (8)
2 eggs
3 tablespoons oil
½ pt/285 ml milk
4 oz/100g flour
seasoning to taste

1. Make the batter with egg, flour, seasoning and milk.
2. Put oil into baking dish and add the sausages.
3. Heat 5 minutes in hot oven (450°F/230°C/Gas Mark 8).
4. Shake or whisk batter again briefly and add to sausages.
5. Bake for 30 minutes in the hot oven until batter is well risen and golden.

The vegetarian Sosmix (see the note following Cheese Burgers in this chapter) may be used in this recipe with good results.

IF YOU HAVE AN OVEN, BAKED POTATOES ARE USEFUL

Preparation & cooking   Wind force: 4
time: 1¼ hours

Wash, dry and grease a large potato for each person, scoring across the top in the form of an 'X'. Cook these in a moderate oven (350°F/175°C/Gas Mark 4) in a deep dish then fill with any of the following, using quantities to suit yourself:

● Take a small slice from base of potato to allow to stand firmly, remove flesh from potato and mash with butter and seasoning plus a pinch of curry powder. Return to shells, place each on foil and pull foil up round the potato, then re-heat – or pack into the oven dish securely so they do not topple over.

Use method outlined above to prepare the following fillings:

● Mix flesh with grated cheese and a pinch of chervil.

● Mix flesh with chopped corned beef and a pinch of tarragon.

● Mix flesh with cream cheese and a pinch of dill or basil.

● Mix flesh with a chopped hard boiled egg and teaspoon of tomato purée.

● Mix flesh with a tiny squeeze garlic purée and some tinned prawns. A small tin should serve four people. Add a little butter or milk.

● Mix flesh with chopped cooked ham, or ham and cheese.

● Mix flesh with drained and mashed tinned salmon. Add a little yoghurt and a pinch of mint if available. A small tin (7 oz/175g) should fill four potatoes.

● Fry a chopped onion, mix with chopped cooked left-over chicken or cheese and the flesh from the potato.

● Mix flesh with grated cheese, a small amount of chopped gherkin and a knob of butter.

● Mix flesh with sardine, tomato purée and a little yoghurt.

● Mix flesh with a large knob of butter and a quarter of a small (7 oz/190g) tin of chopped mushrooms, or creamed mushrooms (in which case omit the butter).

For those who have not previously cooked a baked potato: when it's ready, remove the potato from the oven and slice small piece from bottom as explained above – then squeeze the centre gently with fingers. You will find the top 'X' opens up, allowing easy access to the flesh inside. Spoon this out carefully, to avoid breaking the skin.

A baked potato is cooked when it gives easily when gently squeezed between the fingers – there should be little resistance.

MUM-IN-LAW'S MUSHROOM SCRAMBLE

First invented by her during the war to help eke out the rationing, it has remained a family favourite ever since.

Serves 2   Wind force: 5
Preparation & cooking time: 10 minutes

2 lamb's or 1 pig's kidney
4 slices bacon
4 large mushrooms
4 slices bread
1 × 6½ oz/170g tin tomatoes or 4 fresh,
*   chopped finely*

This dish is so versatile – add or delete items to suit yourself. Prepare kidney early if possible by cutting in half, removing the tough 'core' and the skin. If desired a little roux (see Sauces and Dressings chapter) may be added to give a rich sauce, when added to the pan juices.
1. Prepare kidney as above, slice mushrooms and chop bacon. Prepare tomatoes.
2. Mix all ingredients in deep pan and fry gently till cooked, stirring. Season to taste, adding roux now if desired.
3. Toast the bread and serve the scramble mixture on top.

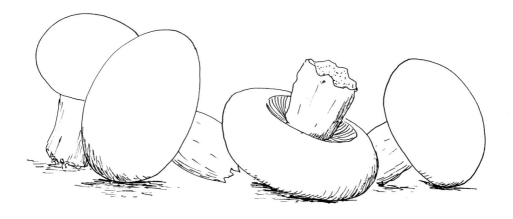

PRETEND PIZZA

Serves 1   Wind force: 5
Preparation & cooking time: 5 minutes

1 slice bread
1 tomato
2 slices cold meat or sardines to suit taste
1 slice cheese
pinch dill or fennel

1. Toast one side of bread. Slice tomato.
2. Lay slices of tomato, cold meat, cheese and herbs on untoasted side.
3. Grill under gentle heat till cheese is melted and the meal thoroughly hot.

   A slice or two of anchovy or some olives may be laid on top if desired.

EGGS IN A PAN

Serves 4   Wind force: 5
Preparation & cooking time: 12 minutes

1 × 7½ oz/190g tin mushrooms
½ oz/15g margarine
6 eggs
pinch dried thyme
seasoning to taste
4 slices cooked ham
2 oz/50g cheese (such as Edam)

1. Open tin of mushrooms and drain. Grate cheese. Chop ham.
2. Beat eggs lightly and season, add thyme.

3. Heat margarine in frying pan and add eggs with the mushrooms and ham.
4. Stir gently, cooking for 4 or 5 minutes and allowing the uncooked egg to run underneath the omelette.
5. Sprinkle cheese on top and flash grill for a moment to melt.

   Serve at once in wedges.

EGGS WITH ASPARAGUS

Serves 4   Wind force: 5
Pre-boil eggs, then
preparation & cooking time: 10 minutes

8 hard boiled eggs
1 small onion
1 oz/25g margarine
1 oz/25g flour
1 × 15 oz/425g tin asparagus soup
4 tablespoons milk
½ teaspoon turmeric
½ teaspoon dill seeds
seasoning to taste

1. Peel eggs, peel and chop onion.
2. Melt margarine and cook onion till soft, stir in flour, dill and turmeric. Cook for 3 minutes, stirring.
3. Remove from heat, stir in soup and milk, blending well.
4. Return to heat and stir till boiling. Check seasoning.
5. Halve eggs, lay in sauce and heat through, turning gently, then serve.

☆
Crack an egg on the inside of a bowl rather than on the edge, thus saving the white from dripping on wrong side.
☆

☆
Tap hard boiled eggs round the middle to crack, then pull the shells gently. Most times they will come apart cleanly.
☆

GOLDEN EYE

Serves 1   Wind force:5
Preparation & cooking time: 5 minutes

> *1 slice bread*
> *2 rashers bacon*
> *1 tomato*
> *oil to cook*
> *1 egg*
> *seasoning to taste*

1. Halve tomato. Cut centre out of bread with tumbler. Heat oil.
2. Fry one side of the bread with bacon slices, tomato and centre of bread.
3. Turn bread over. Break egg into open centre and fry gently till egg is cooked. Serve at once.

BREAD 'N' CHEESE LUNCH

Oven necessary
Serves 3   Wind force: 5
Preparation & cooking time: 35 minutes

> *6 slices stale bread*
> *squeeze garlic purée (1 crushed clove)*
> *2 eggs*
> *½ cup white wine or milk*
> *½ cup chicken stock*
> *8 oz/225g cheese*
> *1 teaspoon Worcester sauce*
> *½ teaspoon made mustard*
> *seasoning to taste*
> *pinch cayenne pepper (to taste)*

1. Spread garlic on bread and crumble roughly into ovenproof dish. Grate cheese and sprinkle on top.
2. Beat eggs and add wine or milk, stock, sauce and all seasonings.
3. Pour all over bread and bake uncovered for 30 minutes in a medium oven (350°F/180°C/Gas Mark 4).

THE GREAT BEAN BINGE

Serves 4   Wind force: 5
Preparation & cooking time: 15 minutes

> *enough left-over potatoes for 4, or 1 packet*
>   *(6 servings/131g) instant potato*
> *1 onion*
> *4 oz/100g bacon*
> *6 oz/150g Cheddar cheese*
> *½ oz/15g margarine*
> *1 × 15¾ oz/447g tin baked beans*
> *dash Worcester or brown sauce*
> *a little milk and butter*
> *seasoning to taste*

1. Prepare and mash potatoes.
2. Peel and slice onion, grate or cube cheese, cut bacon into strips and stow all safely till required.
3. Melt margarine in deep pan. Add onion and bacon and cook till soft, stirring now and then.
4. Add beans, stir and heat. Add sauce and seasoning.
5. Spread in grill pan, sprinkle on cheese and grill to melt.
6. Mix potatoes with a little milk, spread on cheese, dot with butter and grill for a moment or two.

    Serve at once.

☆

Sometimes the ovens on boats tend to be hotter at the back, so it pays to turn oven dishes several times during cooking for an even result.

☆

POTATO CHEESE PIE

Oven necessary
Serves 4   Wind force: 6
Preparation & cooking time: 25 minutes

1½ lb/675g cooked potato (or 6 servings/131g
  packet instant potato)
2 oz/50g margarine
1 × 6½ oz/165g tin tomatoes
3–4 oz/75–100g sharp cheese
1 tin corned beef
seasoning to taste
dash of nutmeg

First prepare ingredients as follows and stow till required:
1. Mash potatoes. Open tins, slice corned beef, drain tomatoes, grate cheese.
2. Mix half the margarine into potatoes and season with salt, pepper and nutmeg.
3. Spoon into ovenproof dish and lay corned beef slices on top.
4. Lay tomatoes on top (drain off some of liquid if very runny), sprinkle on cheese and rest of margarine.
5. Cook in moderate oven (350°F/175°C/Gas Mark 4) for 15 minutes.
  Serve, if desired, with chutney.

☆
Line shelves with thin plastic foam to hold contents still and avoid breakages. Wedge spaces in cupboards (specially those holding glassware) with thicker foam. Empty foam egg boxes work well in an emergency.
☆

CHEESE NESTS

Serves 4   Wind force: 6
Preparation & cooking time: 10 minutes

1 packet (6 servings/131g) instant potato
1 × 15¾ oz/447g tin baked beans
1 × 7 oz/175g tin corn kernels
1 × 7 oz/175g tin tomatoes
1 tablespoon dried onion flakes
4 eggs (weather permitting)
4 oz/100g grated cheese

1. Make up potato as directed on packet. Drain corn and tomato.
2. In non-stick pan (if possible) heat corn, baked beans, tomatoes and onion flakes.
3. Add herbs and cheese. Cook till hot and onion flakes have plumped out.
4. Season. Spoon hot potatoes onto four plates and make a depression on the tops.
5. Spoon the bean mixture into the nests. (Serving is best done one at a time in heavy weather.)
6. Poach or fry 4 eggs and slide onto the top of the bean mixture if weather permits.

Further idea for a topping for the nests. . .

1 onion
oil to cook
1 × 7 oz/175g tin button mushrooms
4 slices sharp cheese
paprika
seasoning

1. Peel and chop onion. Drain mushrooms. Chop up cheese.
2. Lightly fry onions in a little oil in a non-stick milk pan.
3. Add mushrooms and the cheese. Stir till cheese melts. Season.
4. When hot spoon over potatoes as above. Season. Sprinkle paprika on top.

CURRIED EGGS

Serves 2   Wind force: 6
Pre-boil eggs then
preparation & cooking time: 10 minutes

8 hard boiled eggs
1 × 15 oz/425g tin curry sauce
1 heaped tablespoon chutney
pinch chilli powder to taste
2 onions
oil to cook

1. Peel and slice onion, peel eggs.
2. Cook onions in oil till soft.
3. Add sauce and chilli powder, chutney and halved eggs. Heat and serve.

☆

A cube of sugar in the cheese dish will help stop the cheese from going mouldy.

☆

DEVILLED SAUSAGES

Serves 4   Wind force: 6
Preparation & cooking time: 30 minutes

You can help prepare sausages in advance in the following way: part cook the sausages by covering with boiling water, leaving till the water is cold, then draining. When cooking they then only need heating and browning.

1 lb/450g beef or pork sausages (8)
1 teaspoon made mustard
dash cayenne pepper
1 teaspoon vinegar
1 teaspoon piquant sauce (soya/tomato mixed, Worcester etc.)
2 dessertspoons oil
1 packet (6 servings/131g) instant potato
1 packet (4 servings 2.2 oz/62g) peas (or tinned or frozen peas)

1. Cook 8 large sausages under the grill for 20 minutes, turning.
2. Combine all sauces and spices.
3. Prepare potatoes and peas and heat.
4. When sausages are nearly ready brush with spicy dressing and cook a few minutes longer.
   Serve with vegetables.
   Chicken drumsticks or quarters may be substituted for sausages. If weather is really bad, don't despair. The peas can be put into a vacuum flask with boiling water before you begin and will be ready when required, thus avoiding a pan with hot water slopping about.

CHEESE BURGERS

Serves 4   Wind force: 6
Preparation & cooking time: 10 minutes

When 'freshly afloat' and frozen goods are possible the following is a good, tasty and filling snack and is handy to have in mind while you collect your sealegs.

4 × ¼ lb/100g beefburgers
4 slices cheese
4 dashes tomato sauce
large pinch chilli powder or 4 teaspoons chutney or relish
1 large tomato
4 fresh baps

1. Mix tomato sauce with chilli powder, or chutney or relish if using.
2. Grill or fry the beefburgers, spread with mixed sauce.
3. Top with cheese slices and lay each on a bap base.
4. Lay in grill tray and grill for a few moments to melt cheese.
5. Slice tomato into 4 and lay a slice on top of each portion.
6. Place lid of baps on the base mixture and serve.

Sosmix This is a useful and very tasty vegetarian dry mix which makes up easily into a lovely spicy sausage mix which is really handy to have on board. It can be substituted for sausages, beef or hamburgers and used for fillings for buns, or mixed in with other items to be fried, grilled or baked as rissoles etc.

Pancakes are a surprise change for the crew. They may be made beforehand then filled, covered with foil to prevent burning, and re-heated under the grill in most conditions. The pancakes may be kept in foil for 2 or 3 days. (For pancake recipe see Basic Recipes chapter.) Un-filled pancakes can be re-heated by steaming over a plate, covered in foil, or in a moderate oven (wrapped in foil) for about 10 minutes.

IDEAS FOR FILLINGS FOR PANCAKES

Serves as many as you wish Wind force: 6
Pancakes pre-made
Preparation & cooking time: 10 minutes

- Bacon or ham mixed with tin of creamed mushrooms (serve hot)

- Prawns mixed with tin of creamed mushrooms (serve hot)

- Baked beans mixed with chopped ham (serve hot)

- Sweetcorn, mashed potato and ham or bacon (serve hot)

- Tinned mince, peas with sprinkling of oregano (serve hot)

- Chopped hard boiled egg with tin of creamed mushrooms (serve hot)

- Chopped corned beef mixed with tin of creamed mushrooms (serve hot)

- Chopped corned beef mixed with cream or curd cheese (serve hot)

- Mushrooms, bacon and tomatoes, lightly cooked (serve hot)

- Mash left-over potatoes (or reconstitute a packet – size to suit) and add chopped ham, mushrooms, peas, cheese or whatever you have to hand. Add touch of curry powder (serve hot)

- Cream cheese mixed with chopped tinned pineapple (best served cold)

- Left-over chicken, chopped and mixed with curd cheese, or grated cheese (serve hot or cold)

☆
Line your grill pan with foil to save on washing up and, if you have an oven, line the roasting dish also. This saves soaking later.
☆

Sandwiches – or Not?

Dull old sandwich? Are they? What *is* a sandwich? Certainly they are a useful supplement to a sea-cook, either made prior to sailing, dainty and appetising or, more often, thrown together in a rush when the weather turns nasty and you can't face making a meal.

The following ideas cater for all sorts of weather, from the fair to the foul (and I think the sandwich comes into its own most at the extremes of these). Whatever your own thoughts are about sandwiches I feel it is not a bad idea to set off to sea with some sort of sandwich already prepared and firmly wrapped in plastic film (frozen if you like and the filling permits) so that you are not caught napping if the worst comes to the worst.

If you *are* caught out then there are some ideas in the following pages that may help.

Sandwiches are so versatile they need never be dull. They can be made from bread (white, brown or one slice of each), rolls, pitta bread, granary bread, rye bread, pumpernickel, crispbreads: cooked or uncooked, closed or open, large or small: one, two, three or multi-decker . . . the variety is endless.

They are a godsend in an emergency with just a little thought and a few ideas.

TASTY TOAST

Nowadays the electric sandwich toaster is on sale everywhere for use ashore, but it is also possible to buy a small non electric version which can be used on gas stoves or similar.

There are several brand names, my own (which I have had for a great many years) being a 'Taste-T-Toast'. These are not large, easily stowed and can be so useful on a boat. Two pieces of bread are well buttered, placed butter-side *out* on each side of the toaster and a filling placed on one side – just as with the electric variety. The two handles are then brought together and clamped and the sandwich is toasted over the open flame on both sides. It seals itself when cooking and is easily turned out onto a plate with no spillage. I give some ideas below. The filling chosen should fit in with the wind force at the time of cooking.

Enough filling may be prepared at once for all the crew then the 'toasts' made separately. The cooking time is about 5 minutes while the preparation time depends on the filling chosen. Times given below are average.

FILLINGS FOR SEALED SANDWICHES

Serves 1   Wind force: 5–6
                          depending on filling used
Preparation & cooking time:
8–10 minutes

Remember that cheese may be pre-grated, and other ingredients may be made ready before you begin, which makes life much easier. If you like your bacon crisp then fry it before you start to assemble the sandwich.

- Grated cheese and pickles or chutney.
- Grated cheese and chopped onion.

- Grated cheese and sliced or chopped ham.

- Grated cheese and finely chopped bacon.

- Grated cheese and chopped continental sausage of your choice.

- Finely chopped bacon and chopped onion.

- Finely chopped bacon and egg.

- 1 thin slice of ham and egg.

- Baked beans.

- Baked beans and egg.

- Tinned mushrooms in white sauce.

- Yeast extract spread on bread with most of the above.

Try to avoid very dry ingredients as this gives a rather stodgy sandwich. A spoonful of tinned condensed soup is a useful addition.

Sweet ideas

- Apple, puréed or sliced thinly, sprinkled with sugar and cinnamon.

- Apple as above with small dash of yoghurt. Try using babies' puréed apple sauce.

- Curd cheese, raisins, sugar.

Think up more ideas of your own.

FRENCH TOAST

Serves 1   Wind force: 4
Preparation & cooking time: 5 minutes

Version 1 Whip 1 egg in a tablespoon milk with seasoning to taste. Stir in 1 teaspoon made mustard. Remove crusts from a thin slice of bread and dip into the egg mixture, soaking well. Shake off excess of liquid and fry in a little oil on both sides until crisp.

Version 2 Decrust 2 thin slices of bread, sandwich them together with cheese; ham and onion; cheese and pickle; pâté or chopped ham and mayonnaise with pinch of curry powder. Press together well and dip in egg, fry both sides till crisp and golden.

☆

Put a few grains of rice in salt to keep it dry, or keep some silica gel in a bag in the container, drying it now and then in slow oven.

☆

WELSH RAREBIT
(almost a sandwich)

Recipe serves 1 person. Multiply the recipe by the number of crew, mix it all at once, then make the rarebit up person by person and assemble individually in heavy weather.

Wind force: 4

Preparation & cooking time:
10 minutes

½ oz/15g butter
½ oz/15g flour
large pinch chilli powder
2 fl.oz/44 ml beer (or according to stiffness required)
3 oz/75g sharp cheese
seasoning to taste
2 slices bread

1. Make toast. Melt butter and add flour, cook for a moment or two.
2. Add chilli powder and beer and stir in making a fairly stiff roux, then add cheese. Stir till melted, check the mixture is thin enough for your taste. If not stir in a little more beer.
3. Quickly pour over the 2 slices of toast.

SWISS SANDWICH

Serves 1   Wind force: 5
Preparation & cooking time: 10 minutes

1 oz/25g sharp cheese
½ onion
1 slice cooked ham
2 slices bread
1 egg
a little milk

1. Peel and slice onion and grate cheese. Whip egg and milk.
2. Make a sandwich with the bread, cheese, ham and onion.
3. Dip this in the egg and milk, seasoning to taste, and fry on both sides till golden, using just a little oil.

• Toast 2 slices white bread on one side, fill toasted side with ham and cheese, sandwich together and toast other sides.

• Toast 2 slices of bread on one side, fill with cheese, spread with yeast extract and a touch of chutney. Sandwich together and toast other two sides.

• Toast one side of 2 slices of bread, fill toasted side with cooked bacon and mushrooms, sandwich together and toast other sides.

• Messy but delicious . . . Toast 2 slices of bread on both sides. Fill with cooked bacon and fried egg, sandwich together. Serve whole. Egg should still be runny – best eaten with knife and fork.

A sweet version Spread 2 slices of bread generously with jam of your choice, sandwich together, dip in beaten egg and fry quickly.

MORE FRIED OR TOASTED SANDWICHES

Wind force: 4

Croque-Monsieur Cut crusts off two slices of bread. Lay on a slice of ham, some grated Edam cheese and a touch of made mustard. Press together with other slice of crustless bread and dip into egg beaten with a little milk. Fry in hot oil or margarine for 2 to 3 minutes, turning once until crisp outside and the cheese is melting.

• Fill a sandwich with cheese and drained sweetcorn. Dip into beaten egg and fry carefully on both sides till cheese is melted.

• Spread 2 slices of bread with herbed butter, add slice of cheese, sandwich together and fry quickly on both sides.

• Toast 2 slices of brown bread on one side spread with liver sausage and raw onion rings on the toasted side, sandwich together and toast on outsides.

HAMBURGERS

Wind force: 6

Although not strictly a sandwich do not forget the faithful old hamburger which can be easily tarted up by adding relishes, finely chopped onion, sliced tomatoes, fried egg and so on.

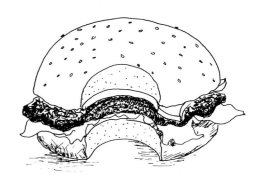

OPEN DANISH SANDWICHES

Suit filling to wind conditions

For each one use 1 slice brown bread, rye bread, crispbread, or pumpernickel with butter, then top with:

● Onion rings, sardines, lemon juice, cress.

● Prawns, lemon juice, mayonnaise and diced celery.

● Prawns, drained tinned grapefruit segments, dash of mayonnaise.

● Liver sausage and scrambled egg.

● Soused herring and onion rings with celery; sprinkled with dill.

● Fold over 2 slices of ham and lay on bread with 1 teaspoon of pickle, lettuce and some cress.

● Prawns, mayonnaise and asparagus.

● Cream cheese topped with prawns and a twist of lemon.

● Crab meat mixed with mayonnaise, olive slices and lemon juice.

● Cream cheese and onion rings topped with cress.

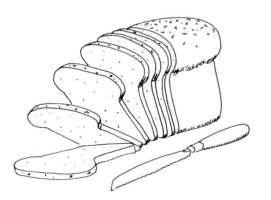

● Sliced hard boiled egg, mayonnaise, a few sprouting beanshoots (see Salads chapter).

● Grated Cheddar cheese mixed with cucumber relish, topped with cucumber slices.

All the above can be easily adapted to be made in rough weather.

SLING TOGETHER DANWICH

Per person   Wind force: 6
Preparation time: 5 minutes

1 slice brown bread, buttered
1 slice ham
few rings raw onion
seasoning to taste
2 tablespoons quark or curd cheese
1 teaspoon chutney
½ apple, sliced and sprinkled with lemon juice

Prepare ingredients first then lay all on bread. Serve with knife and fork if weather allows.

DUTCH UITSMIJTER

Serves 1   Wind force: 6
Preparation & cooking time: 10 minutes

1 slice bread
butter
1 tomato
1 egg (2 for hungry men)
1 slice cooked ham

1. Butter bread and place on plate.
2. Slice tomato, place ham on bread with tomato slices on top.
3. Dry fry an egg (i.e. barely grease pan to stop the egg sticking) and place on top.
4. Serve with lettuce and sliced gherkin on the side.

SANDWICHES

Wind force: Choose to suit wind force

These are listed from about the easiest to prepare down to the more fiddly. Have some fillings prepared for emergencies, then you can spread onto bread fairly easily.

● Brown bread spread with curd cheese, pickle and cress.

● White bread spread with peanut butter and yeast extract.

● Any bread, with mashed corned beef, pickle and sliced onion.

● Wholemeal bread spread with mayonnaise mixed with curry powder to taste, ham and diced cucumber.

● Any bread with grated (or sliced) cheese, pickle, sliced onion.

● Wholemeal bread, sliced tongue, grated (or sliced) Cheddar cheese, sliced onion rings and a few sprouted mung beans (see Salads chapter).

● Brown bread spread with curd cheese, chopped walnut and spring onions cut finely, with sprouted mung beans on top.

● White bread spread with cream cheese, chopped walnut and chopped dates or chopped pineapple. Omit walnuts if desired.

● Brown bread spread with crunchy peanut butter, sliced apple (dipped in lemon juice), a slice of Lancashire cheese and a lettuce leaf.

● Wholemeal bread topped with a mixture of mashed avocado, finely chopped spring onion, pinch of paprika, a lettuce leaf and a slice of tinned or cooked ham.

● 2 × 120g tins drained and mashed sardines, 3 diced hard boiled eggs, teaspoon or so of mayonnaise, dash lemon juice.

● White bread; a 7 oz/198g tin tuna, drained and mashed; 1 chopped onion; ½ green pepper, finely chopped; 2 chopped hard boiled eggs and 6 diced green olives.

● Brown bread with a thin layer of tomato sauce spread over and topped with scrambled egg.

Pitta bread A very handy item to have in your stores locker and one which keeps fairly well for a few days sealed in its packet. Pitta bread may be filled with many varieties of salad, or with hot scramble mixtures. Try some of the pancake fillings, the Mushroom Scramble Recipe (see Lunches, Snacks or Suppers chapter) or the recipe and further ideas below.

BAKED BEANS IN PITTA BREAD

Serves 4   Wind force: 6
Preparation & cooking time: 10 minutes

2 pitta bread
½ oz/15g margarine
1 small onion
½ teaspoon mixed herbs
1 teaspoon made mustard
1 × 7 oz/125g tin baked beans
seasoning to taste
1 × 7 oz/125g tin corned beef

1. Peel and chop onion. Open tins. Cube corned beef. (Prepare above beforehand if possible when weather is threatening to blow up.)
2. Heat margarine in deep pan and add onion. Fry till soft.
3. Add rest of ingredients (except pitta bread) and stir till all are hot.
4. Cut pitta bread in half crossways and open like a paper bag. Fill with above mixture and serve.

The bread may be heated through under grill if desired.

BROWN OR WHITE ROLLS AND PITTA BREAD FILLINGS

Per person   Suit filling to wind conditions

● 1 long crisp roll split, buttered thinly and filled with layers of sliced tomato, sprouted mung beans, onion rings, sweet pickle, lettuce and mashed corned beef.

● Pitta bread halved crosswise and filled with tinned fish mixed with a little mayonnaise and salad.

● Pitta bread halved crosswise and filled with scrambled egg made with a little added grated cheese.

● 1 long crisp roll filled with hot scrambled egg and crisp bacon.

● Pitta bread halved crosswise and filled with chopped cooked chicken mixed with mayonnaise and a dash of curry powder plus a tablespoon of finely chopped onion or pineapple pieces. (This goes well with a salad too.)

● Pitta bread halved crosswise and filled with cold meat and salad.

● 1 soft roll filled with liver pâté, chopped or sliced apple and a dash of Worcester sauce.

● 1 soft roll filled with mashed avocado mixed with a little sour cream (sour the cream with squeeze of lemon juice) and a lettuce leaf.

● 1 round roll filled with mixture of finely chopped ham, pinch of dried chervil, squeeze of garlic purée (or small crushed clove) and bound with thick mayonnaise.

● 1 round roll filled with peanut butter, crisp bacon, crumbled. Add some curd cheese.

● 1 soft roll filled with cream cheese mashed well with chopped dates or pineapple pieces, finely diced.

Season all the rolls or bread to taste and garnish as you wish.

☆

This one is for Himself: When pausing on a painting job (i.e. when called for lunch) wrap the head of your wet brush tightly in plastic film. It will stay soft until you are again ready to use it.

☆

Fish

A fish section in this book is a 'must' if only because there is usually beautiful fresh fish to be had along the coasts of almost any country you visit and if you are sailing you may feel inclined to catch your own as you go.

It is easiest and often tastiest to cook fish as naturally as possible; grilling, frying, cooked as kebabs or coated in flour and basted with butter and/or wine.

However if you are eating a lot of fish, or are not too fond of it, some ideas to ring the changes may be helpful. I include one recipe for frozen fish fingers too that has stood us in good stead over many years as well as a few recipes for tinned fish which is always useful as a stand-by.

Perhaps the recipes will also induce you to try a variety of fish that you may not have met before. More and more new varieties are being sold nowadays, often quite unfamiliar to us. Monkfish (angler fish) for instance may look fearsome but it has a delicate lobster-like flavour which is quite delicious. Do not confuse this with the shark which, in Britain, has the same name.

Also included are some hints on preparing fish and shellfish.

Fish takes very little cooking time, only 5 minutes on the stove for an average fillet. It is delicious cooked simply in the following ways which you could try up to a wind force four at least:

● Made into a thick stew with tomatoes, garlic, carrots, celery, olives, wine, potatoes, stock cube or whatever you have to hand.

● Fried in just a little butter.

● Cooked in cream sauce with wine.

● Fish pie – white sauce, potatoes and cheese topping.

● Lightly crumbed and fried.

● Grilled in butter – brill is specially good cooked in this way.

● Grilled with almonds – use flat fish or trout for this.

● Cooked in a cheese sauce (specially with wine included) – scallops are excellent cooked like this.

● Mackerel go well with gooseberry sauce (can be made with tinned gooseberries).

● Scallops are super fried *lightly* with a little garlic.

To scale fish Use a sharp knife and scrape from tail to head, preferably under running water, but if this is not possible, then in water in a deep basin (use sea water if you wish).

Mussels Tap sharply and immerse in fresh water. Discard any which do not close. Scrape the shell edges clean of debris and pull off any 'beard' protruding from the shell. Cook mussels in boiling water for 2–3 minutes and drain. If any shells are still firmly closed, discard. To cook Mussels Marinière use half water and half white wine, and cook an onion (chopped finely) with the liquid till boiling before adding the mussels.

45

Lobsters There are several schools of thought on how best to kill lobsters but *do not* plunge into boiling water. Either lay in pan and bring gently to the boil or kill the lobster before cooking by plunging the point of a knife into its head where you will find a distinct cross-like mark. This severs the spinal cord and kills it instantly. Cook the lobster in boiling water for about 5 minutes for the first pound in weight and about 3 minutes for each extra pound after that.

All the flesh of the lobster may be eaten except the gills, the intestinal thread (which runs along the back) and a jelly-like sac, all of which are easily identifiable.

Prawns Are often bought cooked, but not always. Cook only for about 2 minutes if raw, before peeling. Pull off the head, squeeze the prawn just where the tail meets the body which will loosen the tail, pull off gently. Turn prawn upside down and prize open between legs, gently pulling off the sections. Wash if dirty.

Crabs As with lobsters, opinions differ as to how to kill a crab, but although I have been told there is a cross on crabs which may be stabbed I have not found it, and think it a dicey business. I feel the kindest way to kill them is to put them into a pan of warm fresh water, which gently puts them to sleep as it warms. I used to plunge them into boiling water till an old Guernsey fisherman pointed out that as these creatures have hard outer shells it takes time for the heat to penetrate enough to kill them, and in the interim they could be suffering agonies. When boiling, cook anything from 5–20 minutes according to size: 15 minutes is about the usual time for a crab the size you would normally buy for two.

To clean, turn crab onto back and push body up where you see a distinct join. Remove gills (grey and feathery, they are well named 'dead men's fingers'). Lever out the bony piece by the eyes and remove the sac attached to it.

Everything else may be eaten. Patience is required to clean out between the bony structures, but often it is most enjoyable to let diners 'do their own thing' – and much easier for the cook. Crab crushers and pickers may be easily bought, worth it if you spend much time in shellfish areas.

Squid These are specially good when small. As they get bigger they are apt to become tough. Wash the squid and gently remove head: often the 'backbone' – an oval, tough and transparent section – will come out too, but if not do not worry. Cut off the tentacles and discard the head (or keep for stock). In Spain the head and tentacles are eaten – certainly the tentacles can be included in the stuffing for the squid. Remove the insides and loosen the backbone gently (if still there). Turn body inside out if large enough and with care scrape off the black skin if any. Wash well. If large enough, the squid can be cut into rings then dipped in batter and fried together with the tentacles. If small, they may be cooked stuffed with the tentacles. There are several other ways to serve them: in Northern Spain, for instance, the speciality is baby squid cooked in their own ink, *Chiperone en su Tinta* – they look dark and unappetising but the taste is really delicious.

Octopus This is often seen in markets, supermarkets or fish shops. Ask when you buy if your octopus has been 'tenderised'. If you are lucky enough to be given a freshly caught octopus ask the donor to kill it for you. You have to bang it on the ground hard until it is dead (somewhat unnerving as it wraps its tentacles round you during the process) or, if you know how, you can fish inside the head and pull out the insides, killing it instantly. This can be hazardous unless you *do* know how as it has a beak with which it can (and, naturally, will) give quite a bite. Once it is dead you have to go through the tenderising process (also if not done before you buy one). To do this you have to hold the creature by the tentacles and either hit it very hard against a hard surface, or throw it onto the quay anything from 60 to 100 times. Don't skimp this or it will be tough. Having tenderised your fish, you then pull out the insides if not already done – be careful not to break the ink sac. Turn inside out and scrape clean, then wash the octopus thoroughly again to get rid of the jelly-like substance covering it. Turn to outside again and wash. This does sound an awful fiddle, but it isn't as bad as it sounds. Having cleaned the creature you may then cook it by boiling, baking, stewing in wine and so on. It takes some time to cook: a knife pushed in should enter easily.

Your octopus may be served as an appetiser, cold with oil and garlic, or crisply fried and served hot; it may go into paella, or be served as a main dish – there are lots of possibilities. It is very good barbecued.

Finally, I have two more points worth bearing in mind. If you can bear it, it is helpful to rub the octopus vigorously against a stone surface just after killing, to remove the 'foam' it will exude, then wash it. If you have a pressure cooker, 20 minutes cooking on high will serve instead of baking and save a considerable amount of time.

If you like seafood and are sailing much, there are two excellent books which I have found most useful: *Fish Cookery* by Jane Grigson and *Mediterranean Seafood* by Alan Davidson (which also covers a great many Atlantic fish).

I have gone into quite a bit of detail on the above because I have so often wished myself that such basic information was handy when I required it.

STUFFED MACKEREL

Serves 4 — Wind force: in port
Preparation & cooking time: — after a successful
stove method: 30 minutes — day's fishing
oven method: 35 minutes

4 large mackerel
2 eating apples
1 small onion
4 oz/100g Cheddar cheese
3 oz/75g margarine
2 oz/50g fresh breadcrumbs
½ teaspoon cayenne pepper
seasoning to taste
oil to cook

Stove method 1. Clean, wash and dry fish. Chop cheese and apples finely.
2. Peel and chop onion finely. Mix half the cheese, apple, onion, breadcrumbs and cayenne pepper together.
3. Season lightly and bind with half the margarine or a little more.
4. Stuff fish and secure edges with toothpicks, dot with remaining margarine and lay in frying pan with a little oil. Cook gently for 10 minutes, turning once. Sprinkle remainder of cheese on top and grill a moment to melt.

Oven method 1–4. Prepare as above but, to cook, lay in baking dish lined with foil, with a trace of oil to prevent sticking.
5. Dot with remaining margarine and bake in a moderate oven (350°F/180°C/Gas Mark 4) for about 20–25 minutes or until tender.
6. Sprinkle remainder of cheese on top and grill in the baking tray for a few minutes to melt cheese – or return to oven.

ANN'S MOCK SALMON DISH

Serves 6   Wind force: in harbour
Preparation & cooking time: 20 minutes plus cooling time (½ hour)

1½ lb/675g white fish
1 × 7 oz/175g tin tuna fish
8 oz/225g tin prawns (optional)
½ pt/285 ml thick mayonnaise
2 oz/50g tomato purée
seasoning to taste

1. Skin fish, steam till cooked, drain and flake. Drain and flake tuna and drain prawns.
2. Mix tomato purée and mayonnaise, mix with the cooled fish and tinned fish, season and put into a deep tin or mould until ready to eat it. Keep in cool place if possible.
    Serve cold with salad and melba toast.

SWEETCORN & SALMON PANCAKES

Serves 4   Wind force 1 & 2
Preparation and cooking time: approx. 1 hour

basic pancake batter (page 22)
1 x 7 oz/195g tin sweetcorn, drained
1 x 14oz/400g tin salmon, flaked, drained and
   deboned
1 x 10 oz/295g tin condensed mushroom &
   pepper soup with cream
half-tsp dried basil
seasoning to taste

1. Make eight pancakes as directed on page 22. Precook if desired.
2. Mix remaining ingredients together.
3. Fold the pancakes into four, in cones. Divide the mixture to fill the pancakes equally.
4. Place in an ovenproof dish and heat through for 20 minutes in a moderate oven (350°F/180°C/gas mark 4).
    Serve immediately with a green salad.

If you like tuna or shellfish then substitute either for the salmon.
    You can add cheese to the mixture before filling the pancakes, or you could sprinkle some over the top before baking.

☆

Ginger is said to be helpful to sufferers of seasickness. Add a little to warm milk and drink slowly.

☆

PEG'S PAELLA

Serves 6   Wind force: 3
Preparation & cooking time: 25 minutes, plus time to cook chicken and rice

3 tablespoons oil
1 large onion
1 large squeeze garlic purée (1 crushed clove)
½ green or red pepper
2 teaspoons mixed herbs (or coriander and
   marjoram)
2 tablespoons lemon juice
4 fl.oz/115 ml water or stock
4 tablespoons tomato purée
4 oz/100g mussels
4 oz/100g prawns
1 lb/450g cooked rice
1 lb/450g cooked chicken or pork
seasoning to taste
1 teaspoon turmeric

1. Clean mussels, discard open ones. Drop them into boiling water for 1 minute then drain. Discard any unopen ones.
2. Chop onion and pepper, clean prawns. Remove mussels from shells, keeping a few in shells for decoration.

3. Cube chicken.

4. Melt oil in a large pan.

5. Add chopped onion and pepper and brown slightly.

6. Mix herbs, garlic and tomato purée to a paste with water or stock.

7. Add to pan then add chicken or pork and simmer gently with lemon juice for 10 minutes.

8. Add rice, mussels and prawns and stir gently. Add turmeric and stir.

9. Season if necessary, decorate with mussels and lemon slices and serve hot.

True paella is made with short grain rice, thus making the dish a little sticky. Long grain may be used to give a fluffier rice.

CRUNCHY HERRING

Oven necessary
Serves 4   Wind force: 3
Preparation & cooking time: 35 minutes
N.B. Clean fish as soon as you buy it.

4 herrings
5 oz/125g potato crisps
1 egg
1 tablespoon water
oil or butter to fry
sprinkling of paprika

1. Coat clean herring in egg beaten with water and then in crushed crisps.

2. Lay on greased baking tray and brush with oil or dot with butter.

3. Sprinkle some paprika over each fish and bake in moderate oven (350°F/180°C/Gas Mark 4) for about 20–25 minutes.

Serve with salad and boiled potatoes.

PRAWN OMELETTE
from *Tasty Dishes with Norwegian Prawns*

Serves 4   Wind force: 3
Preparation & cooking time: 15 minutes

Filling
1/2 tablespoon butter or margarine
1/2 teaspoon curry powder
1 1/2 tablespoons flour
1 1/2 fl.oz/40 ml juice from prawns
  (make up with water)
5 fl.oz/145 ml cream
1 lb/450g peeled prawns
1 small tin asparagus
seasoning to taste

1. Melt butter with curry powder in pan. Stir in flour, add liquid with extra water if required.

2. Reserve 4 asparagus spears for decoration, cut rest into three.

3. Reserve some prawns, add rest to sauce with asparagus. Add cream and heat through well. Season to taste.

Omelette
6–8 eggs
6–8 tablespoons water
1/2 teaspoon salt
1 tablespoon butter

1. Lightly beat eggs and water with the salt.

2. Melt butter in frying pan, pour in the egg mixture.

3. Cook over moderate heat until omelette starts to stiffen.

4. Spread hot filling on half the omelette. Flip over other half. Slide onto plate. Cut into four.

Garnish with prawns and asparagus and serve with lemon wedges and rolls or crispbreads. The omelette mixture may be divided and four separate omelettes made if required.

GEFILTE FISH

Serves 4   Wind force: 3
Preparation & cooking time: 10 minutes and
10 minutes cooling time. Pre-cook eggs.

> *1 lb/¹/₂ kg white fish*
> *1 onion*
> *2 hard boiled eggs*
> *1 apple*
> *1 oz/25g ground almonds*
> *1 egg*
> *seasoning to taste*
> *4 tablespoons oil*

1. Wash, skin and flake fish.
2. Peel and chop onion finely. Peel and chop
eggs and apple. Mix altogether. Add ground
almonds and mix well with seasoning to taste,
bind with egg.
3. Heat oil, fry spoonfuls of the fish mixture for
5–7 minutes, turning.

FISH AND MUSHROOMS

Oven necessary
Serves 4   Wind force: 4
Preparation & cooking time: 40 minutes

> *4 white fish fillets*
> *4 spring onions*
> *2 tablespoons butter*
> *¹/₄ pt/150 ml dry white wine*
> *1 × 7¹/₂ oz/19g tin mushrooms*
> *1 bay leaf*
> *¹/₂ teaspoon chervil*
> *seasoning to taste*

1. Drain mushrooms and chop coarsely.
2. Clean and chop spring onions and clean fish.
3. Mix half spring onions with half the butter (1
tablespoon) and the chervil.
4. Stuff fish with onion and mixture and roll or
fold over.

5. Grease oven dish and sprinkle on remainder
of spring onions.
6. Lay in the fish and season lightly.
7. Toss mushrooms in a pan with ¹/₂ tablespoon
of butter, cook 3 minutes and add wine. Heat
and add to fish with bay leaf.
8. Dot rest of butter over the top (¹/₂ tablespoon)
and cook in moderate oven (350°F/180°C/Gas
Mark 4) for 20 minutes. Baste every so often if
weather permits. If weather is rough, seal with
foil on top (leaving a small steam vent) before
putting into the oven.

QUICK STIR-FRY SEAFOOD

Serves 4   Wind force: 4
Preparation & cooking time: 15 minutes

> *1 small bottle mussels (or about 16 fresh)*
> *7 oz/200g tin prawns*
> *1 × 15 oz/425g tin salmon or tuna*
> *1 small onion*
> *squeeze garlic purée (1 crushed clove)*
> *2 tablespoons margarine*
> *pinch ground ginger*
> *1 × 8 oz/225g packet frozen mixed vegetables*
>   *or peas*
> *2 sticks celery*
> *1 tablespoon cornflour*
> *8 tablespoons dry white wine, cider or stock*
> *2 teaspoons soya sauce*
> *seasoning to taste*
> *4 oz/100g Edam cheese*

1. Drain and flake all fish, reserving liquor of
prawns and salmon.
2. Peel and chop onion, slice celery.
3. Melt margarine in pan, fry garlic, onion and
ginger. Cook 1–2 minutes then add celery and
other vegetables.
4. Add all the fish and stir.
5. Mix cornflour with the wine, cider or stock
and soya sauce as well as reserved fish liquor.

Add to pan and cook for 1 minute, stirring.
6. Slice cheese into strips, or cube, add to pan and stir in. Leave for a moment for cheese to melt. Adjust seasoning.

Serve with pasta or rice.

FELLOWSHIP FISH FINGERS

Serves 4   Wind force: 4
Preparation & cooking time:
stove method: 25 minutes
oven method: 35 minutes

6 oz/150g Cheddar cheese
4 spring onions (or 1 small onion)
1 tablespoon oil
1 × 10 oz/295g tin condensed celery soup
2 large packets fish fingers
1/2 teaspoon paprika
seasoning to taste
1 tablespoon milk

Stove method 1. Grate or chop cheese finely.
2. Clean and slice spring onions, or peel and slice onion finely.
3. Fry onions in oil for 3 minutes. Add fish fingers and fry 5 minutes, turning. Place under grill to keep hot.
4. In a pan, heat soup, paprika, milk and cheese, reserving a little cheese for top. Season to taste.
5. Pour the mixture over the fingers and onions, sprinkle with remainder of the cheese. Grill for a moment to melt cheese.

Oven method 1. Grate or chop cheese finely.
2. Clean and slice spring onions, or peel and slice onion finely.
3. Lay fish fingers in a lightly greased dish.
4. Mix together cheese, soup, milk, paprika and onion, reserving a little cheese for the top.
5. Season lightly and pour over the fish fingers.
6. Bake in moderate oven (350°F/175°C/Gas Mark 4) for about half an hour.

YVONNE'S TUNA CURRY

Serves 2–3   Wind force: 6
Preparation & cooking time: 10 minutes

1 × 7 oz/198g tin tuna
1 × 10 oz/295g tin condensed mushroom soup
1 x 9 oz/250g tin long grain rice (or left-over rice)
1 onion, finely chopped
curry powder to taste

1. Drain and flake tuna, mix with curry powder, soup and finely chopped onion.
2. Heat thoroughly and serve with rice, or fill into pitta bread if desired and eat with fingers.

You could prepare this in almost any wind force as long as your stomachs are secure enough to 'keep down' the rather oily fish.

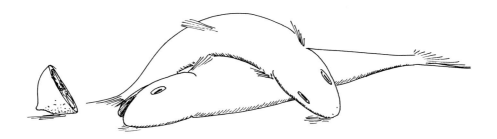

Hot Main Meals

A pressure cooker really proves its worth when preparing meat meals, not only because it is a good, large, deep pan which does not slop liquid but also because it saves times and fuel. It can be used in almost any kind of weather, though if it is dreadfully rough care will be required when coping with the steam.

It is also a boon to those without fridges. Stew or mince (or, indeed, a roast) may be cooked in it, allowed to cool and *left sealed* for at least 24 hours, keeping perfectly well.

It is helpful to remember that most meat dishes can be adapted for pressure cooking if approximately one third the normal cooking time is allowed.

Another use for the pressure cooker is in preparing pasta or rice. The whole is sealed in, even if you do not actually pressure cook the ingredients. The lid fits so well that the likelihood of spills is much reduced.

When using pressure to cook pasta, use plenty of water and salt plus a drop of oil, bring to the boil with the lid on (taking care not to fill the cooker more than two-thirds full) then seal with the pressure gauge and cook for 4 or 5 minutes only depending on the thickness of the pasta. Rice may be tackled in the same way, giving not more than 7 minutes cooking time. Reduce pressure quickly in both cases, but be careful not to scald yourself in the process. Pour off the water before removing the lid completely.

If you are only going on a short trip try to prepare the meat ready to cook before you leave, thus saving time spent in the galley at sea.

Even on longer trips meat and vegetables may be prepared at a convenient time, so that if the weather deteriorates you may spend as little time in the galley as need be . . . it pays to think ahead.

Remember to wedge your cooker in securely; that way you may pop up for a breath of fresh air while you wait for the dish to cook.

It is useful to know, too, that adding curry to meat helps preserve it, and it may then be kept for a longer time.

There are many sauces on the market now, to help make plain dishes more interesting. Do not scorn them – they are very useful not only as a sauce but to make meals more interesting in other ways. For example try spreading some barbeque sauce on pork chops before cooking.

Stir-fry Chinese cookery is admirably suited to boat cooking being quick and liquid free and having the extra advantage that the food will never be over-cooked. It is therefore not only time-saving but nutritious and flavoursome. If planning a 'stir-fry' prepare all the ingredients before you require them. You can then whip up the meal in minutes and in any sea the weather may throw at you.

From the East too comes coconut milk. This is not the liquid inside the nut, but a milk obtained by soaking the grated flesh of the nut in boiling water then squeezing it. It may be bought ready to use in tins (from Asian shops) or in block form (from health food shops as 'coconut cream') and keeps fairly well if wrapped in plastic film. The block should be mixed with boiling water to make the milk. When using the tins mix the milk well to dissolve all the lumps before using. It may be thinned if required. If the prepared milk is not available it can be made by soaking dessicated coconut in a little boiling water, then squeezing it and draining off the resulting milk. This can be repeated perhaps twice, but the result is never as good as from the sources mentioned above. Coconut milk is good in curries and marries particularly well with chicken.

Other useful additions to meals are yoghurt, fresh fruit, butterscotch and chocolate sauces for sweets and some baby foods. For example a little tin of vegetable purée can liven up a soup, or the apple purée (although sometimes a little sweet) provides a useful amount of apple sauce for a meal – you may also sometimes find quite small bottles of purpose-made apple sauce in supermarkets now.

HERBY LAMB KEBABS

Serves 4   Wind force 4
Preparation and cooking time: 30 minutes

1 half-lb leg of lamb cut into one-inch cubes (ask
   your butcher to remove the bone when you buy)
2 medium onions, quartered
4 pork sausages
8 cherry tomatoes
8 medium mushrooms
dried herbs – e.g. sage, oregano, coriander
seasoning

1. Sprinkle lamb cubes with crushed herbs.
2. Prepare onions and put into a bowl. Pour over some boiling water and leave for five minutes. Drain well.
3. Wash vegetable if necessary. Cut each sausage into four.
4. Thread the lamb, sausages and vegetables alternately onto four large or eight small skewers.

5. Season, brush with oil and grill for about 10 minutes until cooked, turning.

This is a good dish to serve the family on your first day at sea. It is excellent with boiled rice and a tasty sauce (bottled if you don't feel like making one yourself). However, if you feel energetic enough you could make a spicy barbecue sauce using tinned tomatoes, a touch of ginger, curry powder or chutney, a spoonful of tomato purée, a chopped apple and seasoning to taste.

A mild curry sauce would also be good. A very spicy sauce would spoil the flavour of the lamb and herbs.

MINTY LAMB

Serves 4   Wind force: 6
Preparation & cooking time: 30 minutes

8 loin lamb chops
8 oz/225g butter
2 teaspoons mint, from a jar
seasoning to taste

1. Rinse mint in water and drain. Wash and trim lamb chops.
2. Mix mint and seasoning with the butter.
3. Spread chops with the butter mixture.
4. Grill or fry 10 minutes on each side.
5. Keep chops hot under grill (weather permitting – otherwise leave in pan) and thin the gravy juices with a little water or stock if necessary.

Serve with mashed potatoes and a salad or vegetable, the gravy poured over the chops.

Herb chops As above, but substitute mixed herbs for the mint.

CHILLI CON CARNE

Pressure cooker recipe
Serves 4   Wind force: 5
Preparation & cooking time: 30 minutes

Using tinned ingredients this could be done in force six or more, but why not make it before you set out, using fresh ingredients, ready to reheat? Then, if bad weather strikes, there will be no hassle at all.

> *1 lb/450g minced beef*
> *1 onion*
> *1 tablespoon oil*
> *1 dessertspoon brown sugar*
> *large squeeze garlic purée (2 crushed cloves)*
> *5 oz/125g tin red pimiento (or 1 sliced red*
>   *pepper)*
> *1 dessertspoon chilli powder (or to taste)*
> *1 × 14 oz/400g tin tomatoes*
> *1 teacup beef stock (½ a cube)*
> *1 tablespoon tomato purée*
> *2–3 dashes Worcester sauce*
> *8 oz/225g red kidney beans (or 1 × 15¼*
>   *oz/432g tin, drained)*
> *left over cooked rice, fresh rice or tinned, to*
>   *suit conditions/availability*

If using dried beans soak overnight in a vacuum flask full of boiling water and cook for about an hour in the morning until tender.

1. Peel and chop onion.
2. Heat oil in pressure cooker and add onion, garlic and chilli powder.
3. Fry till onions are soft and transparent.
4. Add mince and fry till separate and brown, stirring. Add tomatoes and pimiento.
5. Add sugar, tomato purée, stock, beans and Worcester sauce.
6. Cover, bring to boil, place gauge on cooker and bring to high pressure. Cook 10–15 minutes. Reduce pressure slowly. (Leave the cooker in sink for security and have a breath of fresh air.)

7. Check seasoning and that mince is thoroughly cooked. Leave in pressure cooker until ready to eat, reheating if necessary.
   Serve with rice, which, in bad weather, can be mixed in with the meal for ease of serving.

POT ROAST IN A PRESSURE COOKER

Serves 6   Wind force: 3
Preparation & cooking time: 45 minutes

> *1 lb/450g carrots*
> *2 large onions*
> *¾ pt/425 ml stock (1 beef cube)*
> *3 tablespoons oil*
> *3 teaspoons brown sugar*
> *a little flour*
> *2½ lb/1¼ kg topside beef*
> *seasoning to taste*

1. Wash, peel and slice carrots into rings.
2. Peel and slice onion. Make up stock.
3. Wipe meat and rub a little flour over the surface.
4. Heat oil in pressure cooker, add onion, sprinkle with sugar and fry till transparent. Add meat and fry on all sides.
5. Add carrots, seasoning and stock. Bring to boil.
6. Cover and bring to high pressure. Cook for 20–25 minutes depending on how rare you like your meat; 25 minutes will give you a little pink in the centre. If more meat is used allow 10 minutes per lb/½kg extra cooking time. Release pressure quickly.
   Serve with boiled or mashed potatoes and vegetables.

> ☆
> *Carrots will keep fresh if put into paper bags and wrapped in a plastic bag.*
> ☆

BEEF CHOWDER

Serves 4   Wind force: 7
Preparation & cooking time: 10 minutes

2 × 15 oz/425g tin beef stew
1 × 10 oz/275g tin Scotch broth
1 × 7½ oz/190g tin peas
½ soup tin water
½ teaspoon chilli paste or curry powder
1 packet (6 servings/131g) instant potato
water to mix

1. Open tins. Pour soup and beef into deep pan.
2. Add water (if necessary – sometimes there is a lot of gravy with the mince) and drained peas.
3. Mix potato to very stiff paste with water. Add to meat and stir well in with the chilli paste. Heat through, stirring.
   Serve in deep bowls, with crusty bread if desired.

HASTY AND HEARTY

Serves 4   Wind force: 7
Preparation & cooking time: 10 minutes

1 × 12 oz/340g tin corned beef
1 × 15¾ oz/447g tin baked beans
1 × 10 oz/295g tin concentrated tomato soup
1 × 7 oz/175g tin tomatoes
1 × 9 oz/250g tin rice (or pre-cooked rice)
large pinch curry powder
seasoning to taste

1. Break up beef and drain tomatoes.
2. Put all the ingredients except rice into a pan and heat thoroughly. Stir gently all the time. Add rice and heat through.
   This may be served with potato instead of rice.
   When planning to have this dish, remember the tip that tomatoes have been known to make one feel queasy in bad weather, and check with the crew.

GIBRALTAR MOUSSAKA

Oven required (but see note below)
Quantities to suit number of crew   Wind force: 4
Preparation & cooking time: 50 minutes

cornflour
left-over mince (or tinned)
cheese
tomato purée
milk
tinned tomatoes
seasoning to taste
onion (optional)
aubergines (enough to make one layer over
   mince)
potatoes (fresh or dried)
Parmesan cheese (optional)

1. Make a cheese sauce with cornflour, milk and cheese. (See recipe in Sauces and Dressings chapter.)
2. Mix mince with tomatoes (drained) and tomato purée to taste. Season. Add a little lightly fried onion if liked.
3. Peel and slice potatoes (or use packet). Wipe and slice aubergines.
4. Boil potatoes and aubergines till just soft. Drain well.
5. Arrange mince in oven dish, lay vegetables on top in layers. If mince mixture is very sloppy remove a little gravy.
6. Pour over the cheese sauce. Sprinkle with Parmesan cheese if liked.
7. Cook in moderate oven (350°F/180°C/Gas Mark 4) for 30 minutes.
   If you have no oven, this could be assembled quickly as above when still very hot and then browned under the grill as long as all the ingredients were thoroughly cooked and the mince mixture heated through well.

MADRAS MINCE

Serves 4 Wind force: 7
Preparation & cooking time: 10–15 minutes

1 × 15 oz/425g tin mince
1 × 15 oz/425g tin meatballs
1 × 15¼ oz/432g tin kidney beans
1 × 15 oz/425g tin apple slices, drained, or
 sliced fresh apple
4 tablespoons dried onion flakes
1 large teaspoon curry paste or powder
squeeze garlic purée (1 crushed clove)

1. Open tins, drain beans.
2. Place mince, meatballs, curry, garlic and onion flakes in pan and mix.
3. Add beans and apples and mix gently.
4. Heat through gently, stirring.
 Serve with rice, noodles or potatoes.

CHEOY LIN MINCE

Serves 4 Wind force: 6
Preparation & cooking time: 30 minutes

1 onion
a little oil
1 lb/450g mince or 1 × 15 oz/425g tin
1 teacup water
1 beef stock cube
2–3 large dashes tomato sauce
2 large dashes Worcester sauce
3 teaspoons dried mixed herbs
1 dessertspoon dried parsley
1 × 15¾ oz/447g tin baked beans
seasoning to taste

1. Peel and chop onion. Fry gently in oil. Add mince and stir in well.
2. Add all other ingredients except beans. Mix well.
3. Cook slowly stirring occasionally for 15–20 minutes if using raw mince, otherwise heat thoroughly.

4. Add more water if mixture is too dry. Add beans, heat and check seasoning.
 Can be easily adapted to make **cottage pie** by topping with mashed potato. Pop under grill (standing in grill pan for security) for a minute or two to brown.

> ☆
> *Use herbs and spices to perk up tinned meat and fish.*
> ☆

VEAL FRICASSEE

Pressure cooker recipe
Serves 4 Wind force: 4
Preparation & cooking time: 40 minutes

2 lb/1 kg stewing veal
2 oz/50g butter
2 onions
1 oz/25g flour
4 oz/100g mushrooms
5 fl.oz/140 ml dry white wine
1 teaspoon brown sugar
4 egg yolks
salt
1 tablespoon lemon juice
½ teaspoon ground cardamom
8 peppercorns
1 pt/570 ml water

1. Wipe and cut meat into small cubes.
2. Peel and slice onions and mushrooms.
3. Boil onions, sugar, cardamom, salt and peppercorns in water at high pressure for 10 minutes. Release pressure quickly.
4. Add meat and boil at high pressure for 5 minutes. Release pressure quickly. Strain off stock, leave meat and vegetables in sieve.
5. In cooker melt the butter and add flour, blend well.

6. Add half the stock, wine and mushrooms and cook rapidly for 5 minutes.

7. Beat egg yolks with lemon juice and add to stock.

8. Stir gently till thick and creamy, add more stock if too thick.

9. Add meat and vegetables and cook gently till heated through.

Serve with potatoes and broad beans.

MALAYAN CURRIED CHICKEN

Serves 4   Wind force: in harbour
Preparation & cooking time:
25 minutes for the curry plus
about half an hour to prepare the side dishes

Side dishes
1 banana, diced (at last minute)
1 dish dessicated coconut
1 onion, finely chopped and covered with
*   coconut milk*
1 dish mango chutney
½ cucumber, finely chopped and covered with
*   coconut milk*
1 tomato, diced
2 hard boiled eggs, diced
1 dish salted peanuts
prawn crackers
1 small tin pineapple, drained and diced

Chicken curry
1 large tin chicken in jelly or 4 chicken quarters
1 apple
1 teaspoon curry powder (or to taste)
2 × 10½ oz/290g tins curry sauce
8 oz/225g rice
large pinch chilli powder

1. Wash and cook rice.
2. Drain and cut up the chicken, removing bones and reserving the jelly.
3. Peel, core and chop the apple.

4. Put chicken, apple and curry sauce into pan with curry and chilli powder. If fresh chicken is used, cook the chicken in the sauce before adding the apple. (This dish is improved if half a cup of coconut milk is added at this stage.)

5. Heat through for about 10–12 minutes over medium heat, stirring occasionally.

6. If too thick add some of the reserved chicken jelly.

Serve with rice and the side dishes, which are sprinkled on or round the chicken and rice.

Note: Any left over jelly from the tinned chicken can be used in soups.

CHICKEN IN COCONUT

Serves 6   Wind force: 3
Preparation & cooking time: 35 minutes

6 chicken quarters
juice and rind of ½ lemon
1 green pepper
2 onions
2 teaspoons minced garlic
4 tablespoons oil
4 fl.oz/115 ml coconut milk
1 teaspoon curry powder
seasoning to taste

1. Wipe chicken. Squeeze lemon and peel off rind thinly. Sprinkle chicken with lemon juice, curry powder, garlic and seasoning.

2. Peel and slice onions, deseed and slice pepper thinly.

3. Heat oil in deep pan and lay in the marinaded chicken. Fry 10 minutes, turning, till brown.

4. Add onions and fry 3 minutes. Add pepper and lemon rind, cover and cook slowly until vegetables are soft.

5. Add coconut milk. Cover again and cook until chicken is tender. Check seasoning.

Serve with rice, and peas if desired.

CHEESY CHICKEN BAKE

Serves 4   Wind force: 7 – if you are game
Preparation & cooking time: 10 minutes

 2 × 7¹/₂ oz/190g tins supreme of chicken
 1 × 5 oz/125g tin peas (or large (2 oz/62g)
   packet)
 1 × 7 oz/175g tin sweetcorn
 seasoning to taste
 4 oz/100g Cheddar cheese
 1 large packet potato crisps

1. Open tins, drain vegetables, put with chicken into a pan and mix well. If using packet peas, pre-cook.
2. Heat slowly, stirring. Slice cheese.
3. Put hot chicken mixture into grill pan, seasoning to taste.
4. Sprinkle crisps over top, crushing as you go.
5. Lay cheese in slices on top of crisps and heat under grill till cheese has melted.

BARBAREE NASI GORENG

Serves 4   Wind force: 4
Preparation & cooking time: 15 minutes

 2 tablespoons oil
 1 medium onion
 1 × 7¹/₂ oz/190g tin chicken
 1 × 7 oz/175g tin ham
 1 × 7¹/₂ oz/190g tin mushrooms
 1 × 3¹/₂ oz/90g tin crab meat
 1 × 7 oz/175g tin prawns
 1 × 7¹/₂ oz/190g tin peas
 3 teaspoons soya sauce
 8 oz/225g (approximately 2 cups) cooked rice
 4 eggs (optional)
 gherkins to garnish

1. Open and drain tins. Peel and dice onion. Cube chicken and ham.
2. In deep pan heat the oil and fry onion till soft.
3. Add all other ingredients except rice. Toss with slotted spoon till hot. Add rice, mix well and heat through thoroughly, turning. If weather permits fry an egg for each person and top the Nasi Goreng with it before serving. Garnish with gherkins, sliced in a fan shape.
   'Nasi Goreng' is Malay for 'fried rice'.

CHINESE CHICKEN WITH PINEAPPLE
from *How to Cheat at Cooking*

Serves 4   Wind force: 4
Preparation & cooking time: 30 minutes

 oil and butter
 1 medium onion
 4 oz/100g cooked green beans, canned or
   frozen
 1 level tablespoon soft brown sugar
 squeeze garlic purée (1 crushed clove)
 1 tablespoon flour, seasoned with salt and
   pepper
 1 lb/450g cooked chicken
 1 level tablespoon cornflour
 1 × 13 oz/375g tin pineapple chunks
 3 tablespoons malt vinegar
 1 × 7¹/₂ oz/190g tin grilling mushrooms
 seasoning to taste

1. Peel and slice onion, dice chicken, drain and chop mushrooms.
2. Heat a little oil and butter in pan and gently fry the onion till soft.
3. Toss chicken pieces in seasoned flour (shake in a bag or box).
4. Stir chicken pieces into onion. Cook 10 minutes, stirring occasionally. Keep heat low.
5. Drain pineapple and reserve juice. Add pineapple to chicken.
6. Add mushrooms and beans. Stir again, keeping heat low.
7. Mix brown sugar and cornflour into a paste with the vinegar.

8. Add pineapple juice and pour it all into the pan.

9. Turn heat up and bring to the boil, stirring all the time.

10. Check seasoning and simmer gently for another 8 minutes.

Serve with rice or noodles.

In her book Delia Smith warns against being put off by the number of ingredients . . . please take note of this: the dish is very easy to make.

☆

Wine in cooking adds interest to stews, as do tinned mushrooms or tomatoes.

☆

ROS ARCAN THIS AND THAT

Quantities to suit size of crew   Wind force: 4
Preparation & cooking time: 20 minutes

left-over cooked pork or chicken
bacon slices
soaked prunes
butter
onions
flour
garlic
wine
¼ teaspoon ground cinnamon
yoghurt
seasoning to taste

1. Cube meat, peel and slice onions, cut bacon into strips.

2. Stone prunes, crush garlic. Melt butter and cook onion. Add garlic and cook 2 minutes. Add flour and cook gently, stirring, for 3 minutes. Add wine gradually to make a stiff roux.

3. Add all other ingredients except yoghurt and seasoning. Cook over low heat till thoroughly hot. Check seasoning.

4. Add yoghurt to taste and fold in gently.

VIERGE CHICKEN

Oven necessary
Serves 4   Wind force: 6
Preparation & cooking time: 1 hour 35 minutes

4 large portions chicken
2 teaspoons garlic purée
seasoning to taste
1 teaspoon paprika
2 × 7½ oz/190g tins mushrooms
1 × 10 oz/295g tin condensed cream of chicken soup
1 cup cream

1. Wipe chicken portions. Mix garlic, seasoning and paprika.

2. Rub the spice mixture into chicken. Place in baking dish.

3. Drain mushrooms and sprinkle on top of chicken.

4. Dilute the soup with the cream. Pour over chicken.

5. Bake, uncovered (or loosely covered with foil in bad weather – allowing a small steam vent) in moderately slow oven (300°F/150°C/Gas Mark 2) for 1–1½ hours, till tender.

PLEASE YOURSELF PORK

Quantities to suit size of crew   Wind force: 5
Preparation & cooking time: 35 minutes

fillet of pork
onions
peppers
mushrooms
tinned condensed mushroom soup
generous dash of paprika
herbs of your choice
rice
frozen peas
oil to cook

1. Clean and cook rice and keep hot in the pan as in Chinese method (see Basic Recipes chapter).
2. Peel and chop onions. Clean and chop peppers and mushrooms.
3. Cut pork into small cubes or slices.
4. Fry pork in a little oil for 5 minutes, turning. Add onion.
5. Fry 1 minute and add peppers and mushrooms. Fry 1 minute.
6. Add soup, herbs and paprika.
7. Simmer till infused, stirring occasionally.
8. Add peas when pork is tender and heat it all through well.
   Serve with the rice.
   This is not difficult if you tackle each part in turn and stow safely, perhaps in the sink in a bowl, until required.

☆
In good weather several tins may be opened and heated together in one pan of water to save space and fuel.
☆

PORK CHOPS WITH MUSTARD

Serves 4   Wind force: 4
Preparation & cooking time: 30 minutes

4 loin pork chops
1 tablespoon margarine and oil
1 dessertspoon orange juice
1/4 pt/140 ml red wine
1 tablespoon made mustard
1 small carton natural yoghurt
seasoning to taste

1. Wipe chops, season and fry in margarine and oil till cooked, turning – about 15-20 minutes, depending on size.
2. Remove chops from pan and keep hot.
3. Add orange juice and wine to juices in pan, bring to boil.
4. Stir until reduced slightly. Remove from stove.
5. Stir in mustard and yoghurt, return chops to pan and heat.

LUNCHEON MEAT WITH BACON AND BEANS

Serves 4   Wind force: 4
Preparation & cooking time: 15 minutes

1 × 12 oz/350g tin luncheon meat
8 oz/225g streaky bacon
1 × 15³/4 oz/447g tin baked beans
4 slices tomato
scant teaspoon thyme
2 tablespoons oil

1. Cut luncheon meat into 8 slices.
2. Stretch bacon rashers, removing rind.
3. Slice tomatoes and open the tin of beans.
4. Wrap bacon round meat and fry gently for 10 minutes in oil, turning.
5. Add and fry tomato slices.
6. Heat beans in another pan with thyme.
   Serve with noodles or mashed potatoes.

BOILED HAM

Pressure cooker recipe
Serves 6   Wind force: 4
Preparation & cooking time: 55 minutes

3 lb/1½ kg ham
6 peppercorns
1 onion
water

1. Cover ham with water in the cooker and bring to boil. Drain.
2. Cover again with water.
3. Peel onion, add with peppercorns to the ham.
4. Boil at high pressure for 40 minutes. Release pressure quickly.
5. Drain and serve with boiled potatoes, butter beans and mustard.

☆
Tinned and packet soups added to fresh minced meat and mashed potatoes make good sauces.
☆

COOKED HAM IN CHEESE SAUCE

Serves 4   Wind force: 5
Preparation & cooking time: 10 minutes

¾ lb/350g cooked ham
1 onion
1 oz/25g butter
1 oz/25g flour
½ pt/285 ml milk
4 oz/100g mature Cheddar cheese
seasoning

1. Peel and chop onion, cube ham.
2. Melt butter in pan and add flour, make roux with milk (see Basic White Sauce recipe in Sauces and Dressings chapter).
3. Cube cheese and add to roux.
4. Add ham, stir and heat gently for 5 minutes.
5. Season to taste.
   Serve on toast or with mashed potatoes.

NAZEBY LEFT-OVERS

Serves 4   Wind force: 5
Preparation & cooking time: 15 minutes

1 large onion
1 oz/25g butter
1 × 14 oz/400g tin tomato or tomato juice
1 tablespoon tomato purée
dash Worcester sauce
pinch paprika or cayenne pepper
1 tablespoon cornflour
seasoning to taste
any left-over cubed meat or tins of ham,
   meatballs etc.

1. Peel and chop onion, fry in fat till soft.
2. Add rest of ingredients except cornflour and meat. Heat.
3. Mix cornflour with a little water and add, stirring.
4. Add meat as desired and heat well. Check seasoning.

ROGNONS MARITIMES

Serves 4   Wind force: 3
Preparation & cooking time: 30 minutes

12 lamb's kidneys
2 medium onions
fat to fry
heaped teaspoon curry powder
1 packet frozen mixed vegetables
1 tablespoon flour
¼ pt/140 ml milk
seasoning to taste

1. Clean, core, skin and halve the kidneys. Peel and chop onions.
2. Fry onions in fat till transparent.
3. Add kidneys and curry powder and fry 2 minutes, turning.
4. Add milk, reserving 2 tablespoons, and stir in; cook slowly for 10 minutes, stirring occasionally.
5. Mix flour with the extra milk and seasoning. Add to kidney mixture. Cook through for 3 minutes.
6. Add vegetables and heat through. Add a little more milk if necessary.
   Serve with spaghetti.

TIDDLY KIDDLY

Serves 4   Wind force: 4
Preparation & cooking time: 15 minutes

8 lamb's kidneys
6 oz/150g mushrooms
1 large onion
1 oz/25g margarine
3 tablespoons yoghurt
1 tablespoon dry sherry
seasoning

1. Clean, core, skin and slice kidneys.
2. Clean and slice mushrooms, peel and slice onion.

3. Heat fat in a pan and add kidney. Cook 1 minute.
4. Add the onions, cook for 5 minutes. Add mushrooms, cook 3 minutes more, stirring.
5. Add yoghurt and sherry, heat through and check seasoning.

STIR-FRY LIVER AND BACON

Serves 4   Wind force:3
Preparation & cooking time: 15 minutes

2 medium onions
8 mushrooms
1½ lb/675g lamb's liver
4 large rashers bacon
1 tablespoon oil
2–3 teaspoons soya sauce
½ teaspoon made mustard
1 small tin garden peas (or fresh/frozen if
  available)

1. Peel and slice onions. Clean and slice mushrooms.
2. Wipe and slice liver *thinly*. Derind bacon and cut into thin strips.
3. Drain peas.
4. Pour oil, soya sauce and mustard into frying pan.
5. Add onions and stir-fry for 2 minutes. Add liver and fry 2 minutes more.
6. Add bacon and mushrooms, fry 1 minute, stirring and tossing.
7. Add peas and heat through quickly. The liver should be pink inside and very tender.
   To stir-fry just means to fry quickly over a high heat while tossing and turning the ingredients the whole time so they do not stick or burn. The fact that the food is thinly sliced allows for very quick cooking. Adding more oil should not be necessary but if the pan looks very dry a little can be poured in.

The following are four main-meal sauces to serve with pasta:

TUNA SAUCE

Serves 4   Wind force: 3
Preparation & cooking time: 10 minutes

2 sticks celery
2 onions
2 × 7 oz/198g tins tuna fish or salmon
1 tablespoon oil
½ teaspoon cayenne pepper
1 tablespoon cornflour
water to mix
1 × 5 oz/125g carton plain yoghurt
seasoning to taste

1. Clean and cut celery into ½ in (1 cm) pieces. Peel and chop onions.
2. Drain fish and set aside.
3. Cook celery and onions in oil till soft.
4. Add tuna and stir a moment or two to heat. Add cayenne and stir in.
5. Mix cornflour with a little water. Add this with the yoghurt to the fish mixture and heat very gently. Stir till hot and the sauce has thickened and the cornflour is cooked, about 3 minutes.
6. Check seasoning and serve at once.

TOMATO SAUCE FOR SPAGHETTI

Serves 4   Wind force: 4
Preparation & cooking time: 40 minutes

1 tablespoon oil
seasoning to taste
1 onion
1 clove garlic
1 lb/450g tomatoes
pinch dried basil
½ teaspoon curry powder
a little sugar (optional)

1. Peel and chop tomatoes, onion and garlic.
2. Fry onion, garlic and curry powder till soft, in the oil.
3. When the onion mixture is ready, add tomatoes, basil and seasoning.
4. Simmer for 30 minutes. Clamp pan to stove and cover with lid or foil with small steam vent in it, in rough weather. Add a little sugar if desired.
5. Meanwhile cook spaghetti, drain, pour hot sauce over and serve with Parmesan cheese sprinkled over it.

   If the weather permits the dish will be better if you skin the tomatoes before cooking but no harm will come if you leave skins on. If it *is* rough and you really dislike skins in the sauce then you could, at a pinch, sieve the mixture before pouring over the spaghetti. Or make it beforehand, sieve then reheat when required.

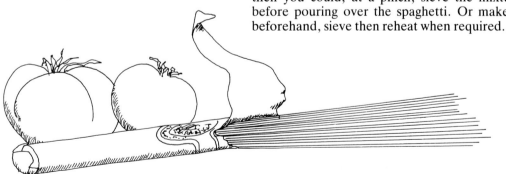

TOMATO SAUCE WITH HAM

Serves 4   Wind force: 5
Preparation & cooking time: 15 minutes

> *2 onions*
> *large squeeze garlic purée (2 crushed cloves)*
> *4 tablespoons oil*
> *1 × 7½ oz/190g tin ham*
> *2 × 15¾ oz/447g tins tomatoes*
> *seasoning to taste*
> *1 large teaspoon dried basil*

1. Peel and chop onions. Dice ham.
2. Fry onions and garlic in oil till soft, in deep pan.
3. Open tomatoes – if very liquid pour some off and reserve. Add the tomatoes with all the other ingredients to the onion mixture.
4. Cook gently for 12 minutes, stirring often, till fairly thick. Add the extra liquid from the tomatoes if necessary, otherwise use in soup later.
   A tin of baked beans may be added if you have a large, starving crew.

BOLOGNAISE SAUCE

Serves 4   Wind force: 5
Preparation & cooking time: 10 minutes

> *2 large onions*
> *squeeze garlic purée (1 crushed clove)*
> *6 tablespoons oil*
> *2 × 15 oz/425g tins minced beef*
> *1 heaped teaspoon curry powder*
> *seasoning to taste*
> *1 × 6½ oz/170g tin tomatoes*

1. Peel and chop onions. Fry in oil with garlic till soft, in deep pan.
2. Add meat and curry powder. Heat well, testing for seasoning. Add tomatoes but if the mince mixture looks runny drain off some of the tomato juice before adding to the meat and reserve to add to soup later. Heat the mixture well, stirring.

☆
Wrap perishables and dry goods first in foil then in plastic film before stowing.
☆

A FEW MORE IDEAS

Wind force: Use an idea to
suit . . . up to force 6 or so

Use these ideas when you have meat in stock and are not sure how to cope with it when the weather pipes up unexpectedly, or try them just for a change.

Beef . . . Stew – add tomato, mushrooms, flageolet beans (tin) with teaspoon horseradish sauce, or add sour cream and paprika. The meat can be coated in seasoned flour (do this in a bag), then transferred to a deep pan, seared in oil and the rest added. Add chopped onion for extra flavour.

Chicken . . . Fried, but first coated in mixture of honey and curry powder (do this in a deep dish) or cooked with tin of unsweetened pineapple pieces.

Chicken . . . Casserole – use tinned soup as sauce and bulk out with walnuts, almonds, pine nuts or cook in some orange juice (tin or carton).

Chicken . . . Portions – super done in cream sauce with raisins, pineapple pieces, handful of pine nuts, teaspoon curry powder.

Chicken . . . Breast – slit open, stuffed with raisins, camembert and chopped apple, breaded and fried, served with a sauce made from tablespoon cornflour, mixed with 2 tablespoons orange juice. Heat slowly and add water till sauce is of good consistency. Add a scant dessertspoon sugar.

Ham...Steaks – try rubbing with mustard and frying in a little fruit juice for a few minutes.

Lamb...Chops – cooked with sauce of natural yoghurt, diced cucumber and chopped onion.

Lamb...Chops – grill with a little butter on top, turn, sprinkle with rosemary and cook till done.

Lamb...Cooked – heat with a white sauce made with onions, sherry and made mustard or use a tin or packet of ready-made white sauce. Perk up if desired with chopped onion, sherry etc. as above.

Pie...Mince – bulk out for a change with chopped apple or porridge oats, tomato or crushed cornflakes to top instead of potato.

Pork...Chops – rub with ground ginger and garlic purée before grilling.

Steak...Slice thinly and stir-fry quickly with a small tin of drained prawns added.

Veal...Escalope – made Cordon Bleu style. For this, make a slit in the side of the slice, insert a slice of cheese, dip the slice in egg and breadcrumbs and fry in a little margarine.

Veal...Stewing – made with sour cream sauce. For Stroganoff add tomato purée, paprika and lemon juice.

☆

If you have to coat meat in flour/seasoning mixture, use an empty margarine tub (or similar) with the lid on to shake it together – or a plastic bag will do. This keeps mess to the minimum. Do not keep used mixture for long though: the meat particles retained in it will go off quickly.

☆

Tinned ready-made sauces Are a useful stand-by, specially in rough weather. If you have meat ready to cook and the weather turns nasty, it is easy to open a tin of sauce, mix in with the meat, add a little herb, spice, curry or garlic to it if you wish, and cook it all together. In these conditions tinned vegetables and reconstituted potatoes speed up the cooking process even further – the crew is fed and happy and the cook is less likely to feel seasick. The trick is in adding that little extra to make the meal tasty and 'different'.

☆

Meat is preserved by currying it, so it may be left safely in a plastic film covered bowl for a day unrefrigerated in warm weather.

☆

FORCE SEVEN STAND-BYS

Preparation & cooking time: approximately 10 minutes

All the following may be cooked in one pan. All should serve four, but take into account the crew's appetite and add a little extra something if desired.

● 2 × 15 oz/425g tins meatballs, drained; 1 tin red wine sauce and, if possible, a chopped onion (or onion flakes).

● Frankfurter sausages (2 per person) cut into bite sizes and simmered with a tin of ready-cooked tomato sauce, with some basil stirred in.

● Left-over chicken, or a tin of chicken in jelly, broken up and mixed with a tin of white wine sauce and some grapes, or leave out grapes and add 4 oz/100g crumbled cheese – this need not be accurately measured at all.

• Left-over rice and a tin of drained peas, plus pinch curry powder, 1 tin roughly chopped luncheon meat and 1 tin drained sweetcorn. Heat slowly in a pan with a little water and a drop or two of oil to prevent sticking. Add a little more during heating, if necessary.

• Left-over chicken, or 1 tin of chicken in jelly, mixed with 1 packet dried peas and 2 slices of bacon, cut up, plus 1 tin of red wine sauce.

• Left-over chicken or 1 tin of chicken in jelly, mixed with raisins, a sliced banana and a tin of curry sauce. Make up a packet of savoury rice to serve with this.

• 1 tin sausages with 1 tin drained peas, 1 tin drained tomatoes and 1 tin curry sauce or goulash sauce.

• 1 large tin pork luncheon meat, roughly chopped and mixed with 1 tin of sweet and sour sauce, plus 1 tin of drained flageolet beans.

• 1 tin ham, roughly diced and mixed with a tin of drained butter beans and a tin of barbeque sauce plus a tin of drained pineapple chunks.

• 1 tin beefburgers with 2 sliced onions and a tin of concentrated tomato soup plus a tin of carrots, drained and chopped up.

• 1 large tin pork luncheon meat, roughly diced and mixed with slices of celery and a tin of goulash sauce.

• 2 tins mince heated up with a packet of savoury rice and a tin of goulash sauce or curry sauce. Top with banana, raisins, nuts etc. as to hand. Make up the savoury rice before you begin.

• 2 tins beef (drained if very liquid) and mixed with small tin sweetcorn and a tin of goulash sauce.

• 2 tins beef (drained if very liquid) and mixed with a small tin of carrots (drained and chopped), a small tin of drained peas and a tin of red wine sauce.

• 2 tins beef (drained if very liquid) and mixed with 1 tin tomato and onion sauce and a drained tin of butter beans.

• 2 tins beef (drained if very liquid) and mixed with 1 small tin tomatoes (drained), a tin of mushrooms (drained) and a tin of red wine sauce.

• 2 tins mince (drained if very liquid) and mixed with 1 tin drained tomatoes, pinch marjoram and a spoonful of dried onion flakes.

All these (except rice dishes) may be served with chunks of bread if desired.

Keep the gravy drained from tins in a screw top or plastic jar and add to tinned or packet soups for extra flavour. The plastic bottles in which you buy dried milk are good for this: scald before and after use in very hot but not boiling water. (Boiling water may cause them to collapse.)

Vegetables

HOW TO COOK SOME COMMON VEGETABLES

Clean vegetables and slice root variety. If you slice thinly they will cook more quickly. Shred **cabbage** and cut **cauliflower** into florets. Remove outer leaves from **brussels sprouts** and cut a cross into the base of each sprout; this facilitates faster cooking. Leave **spinach leaves** whole. Remove outer leaves from **corn on the cob**.

Most **pulses** (dried beans, peas, lentils etc.) should be brought to the boil then left for 12 to 24 hours before cooking. Pulses require quite a long cooking period, and it should be noted that **red kidney beans** *must* be boiled for at least 15 minutes (which in any case they will need to allow them to soften) as they contain a poison which is removed by cooking for this time.

In general it is best to cook most vegetables as quickly as possible and to do so covered. However **brussels sprouts** are best left uncovered. Time taken to boil vegetables should be about 10–20 minutes. To test, push a sharp pointed knife into them: if it slides in easily they are ready. Test frequently so they do not become overcooked.

☆

At sea, when water is clean, use salt water to clean vegetables and half salt/half fresh water to cook them. Do not boil vegetables in pure salt water, it is far too salty.

☆

Spinach should be *gently* cooked for about 5 minutes, covered, but with no water added. Drain very well, squeezing if possible (and if you can, keep the liquid for stock to add to soups as it is both flavoursome and full of vitamins). Chop the spinach and drain again, then add a knob of butter, salt and pepper.

With **cabbage** and **leeks** I think it is much nicer to sweat rather than boil. For this you melt a large knob of butter in the pan, add the vegetables with a little salt and pepper and toss well, then cook over a very low heat, covered, until tender. It is important to cover them. Cabbage will only take a few minutes, while leeks take about 6–8 minutes. Stir once or twice or shake pan with lid on, to prevent sticking.

Corn on the cob, with the outer leaves and silky threads removed, can be placed straight into boiling water and boiled for about 6 minutes, then tested with a knife. However, it is better if steamed (well wrapped in foil) over boiling water, though obviously the weather conditions would dictate whether this could be done. It is also good steamed in the oven, again wrapped in foil, but of course it will take longer.

Do not peel **mushrooms** unless very messy. Wipe and dry on kitchen paper. They are best sautéed for about 3–4 minutes in a mixture of butter and margarine or oil (the mixture stops the butter burning so easily) in an uncovered pan. This should be shaken gently and frequently, or the mushrooms stirred, to prevent burning. Alternatively, grill gently with butter.

French beans, which are small and tender,

should only be topped and tailed before washing, but **runner beans** usually require 'stringing' as well. This entails peeling down each side to remove the tough stringy fibre often found there.

Do not cut up **onions** before boiling and, of course, if you are adding them to stews, mince or other dishes, they are best chopped then fried gently until transparent. If you are cooking **beetroot** (which takes a very long time – perhaps an hour – even when young) wash it but do not peel it until after it is cooked or it will lose its colour.

☆

To chop up an onion without tears, cut the whole onion in half lengthways, including root. Pull off skin but leave root. Make several cuts lengthways from end to end, leaving root intact then cut across, holding the root end with fingers. This helps eliminate watering eyes and is neat.

☆

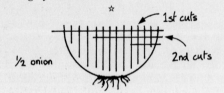

Add a little salt to vegetables before boiling, but not much as it can make them tough. Better to add more to taste when cooked. In bad weather you will not particularly wish to boil, in which case, if you are in a position to cook vegetables at all, you may cook them in several other ways. If you have a pressure cooker, (which should be clamped firmly to the stove if rough) then do the vegetables in that using the manufacturer's instructions. Or stir-fry them, but if using this method first slice them into small strips so they only take seconds to cook in a little

hot fat (*not* enough to spill) tossing frequently. Alternatively you can bake, in which case slice fairly small and put into casserole with a little seasoning and a good lump of butter and cover. Again you will have to make the knife test to ascertain when they are ready, but it will take longer than boiling. Finally, if you know the weather is going to be rough, you can – early in the morning – place the vegetables in a wide-necked vacuum flask, cover with *boiling* water, and leave them until you require them. Then test if tender; if not, a very little more cooking will be required (method of your choice).

Tomatoes are really not good boiled, but if you want cooked tomatoes as a vegetable then you can grill, bake, fry or steam them. If you want to skin them easily, dip into boiling water for about a minute then remove and peel. You will find the skin comes off easily.

Although you will not be worrying too much with fancy vegetables in heavy weather, I have included a few ideas to make them more interesting.

It is also useful to know what to do with some slightly less well known vegetables so I have given a few tips to help cope with these.

UNUSUAL VEGETABLES

Aubergines Sometimes known as **eggplant**. They are now fairly wide-spread and well known; pear shaped, purple vegetables. They are best wiped, peeled (if desired, but not necessary), sliced or cubed and each piece sprinkled with a little salt. Leave them in a bowl to 'sweat' for half an hour or so. Rinse and pat dry in kitchen paper. They may then be boiled, baked, fried, added to moussaka etc. Choose firm, unwrinkled specimens.

Celeriac A root rather like a large wrinkled swede but is white inside and has a celery-like flavour. It may be used in salads (see Salads chapter) or cooked in boiling water, cubed, sliced or cut into matchstick pieces. When cooked in cubes it is delicious mashed with butter. It is cooked when a fork slides into the slice easily.

Fennel This has an aniseed-like flavour and looks rather like a fat head of celery with feathery green fronds. Choose fat, firm bulbs. Slice off tops and base and wash. Slice into even pieces (or peel apart and use separate stalks) and use raw or cooked like celery. Good braised in butter.

Kohlrabi This is like a turnip with leaves growing from the bulbous root. Treat like turnip but it is best steamed rather than boiled.

Salsify Sometimes known as **oyster plant**. Looks rather like a thin parsnip and has a delicate flavour. Peel and if very large cut in half lengthways. Cook in boiling, salted water till just tender, drain and toss in butter.

Radish Long white. This variety, also known as **mooli**, is becoming more popular now. Peel and cube it and serve with cubes of cheese as a pre-dinner snack with drinks, or grate it into a salad.

Samphire A green twiggy plant found in salt marshes. You can pull it from river and mud flats in Northern Brittany. If it is very young and tender you can eat it raw with melted butter – dip it in the butter and strip off the flesh with your teeth, leaving the stringy twig cores. If larger, boil briskly for 5 minutes in *unsalted* water, drain and eat as a starter or vegetable, with butter as above. It has quite a distinctive flavour with no need for additional salt.

Globe artichokes A bit frightening on first confrontation. Some people love them, some hate them. Here is how to cope with them. One head per person is plenty. Choose those which are firm and plump with stiff leaves. Cut off the stem close to the base of the leaves and also about an inch off the top. Soak upside down in fresh salted water for 30 minutes. Beware – cut portions darken easily so if you intend to leave the vegetable about for a while coat with lemon juice.

Cover the artichokes with boiling salted water into which has been poured 1 teaspoon vinegar or lemon juice to each 2 pints of water. Place the vegetables into the water upside down and cook for about 30 minutes. Test by pulling the leaves; if they come out easily they are ready to eat. Drain upside down. Serve with melted butter. Remove the outer leaves and eat the rest by dipping in the butter, then pulling the base of the leaf through the teeth to strip it of its flesh. When you reach the centre scrape off the furry 'choke' and discard; it is uneatable. Then eat the base with a knife and fork.

Jane Grigson's *Vegetable Book* gives many interesting ways to cope with these and other vegetables other than as above.

Jerusalem artichokes Brown, knobbly potato-like tubers. Peel and boil as for potatoes and, like them, test with fork to see if they are tender. Drain well and melt some butter on top of them.

One vegetable to beware of is the most attractive red and white striped **'Runner' beans** you often come across in French markets and other Mediterranean countries. I have found them to be extremely tough, requiring a very long cooking period. Such a pity, they are *so* pretty.

POTATO FLATTIES

Serves 6   Wind force: 3
Preparation & cooking time: 15 minutes

2 lb/1 kg potatoes
1 large onion
2–3 eggs
3 tablespoons oil
seasoning

1. Peel and grate potato and onion, add seasoning and mix with beaten egg to give fairly soft but workable consistency.
2. Drop dessertspoons of the mixture into hot oil in frying pan, flatten and cook till brown on both sides. Make a few at a time and keep hot under a low grill.

These are better made thin, as they are then good and crisp, so add a little more egg if necessary to ensure a soft mixture.

POTATOES ANNA

Serves 4   Wind force 3
Preparation and cooking time: 1 hour 45 minutes

1.5 lb/675g potatoes
2 cloves garlic, peeled and crushed
12 oz/350g onions
1 tin cream
1 oz/25g margarine
seasoning to taste
chopped parsley
grated zesty cheese

1. Peel and slice potatoes and onions thinly.
2. Arrange in layers, with garlic, in a buttered dish. Sprinkle parsley and seasoning over each layer.
3. Stir cream and pour over the potato mixture. Dot with butter and sprinkle with cheese.
4. Cover with foil and bake for 75-90 minutes at 400°F/200°C/gas mark 6. Remove foil for the last 15 minutes.

Serve with a roast to make the most of the oven.

CREAMY TURNIP MASH

Serves 4–6   Wind force: 3
Preparation & cooking time: 25 minutes

1 lb/½ kg swede
1 lb/½ kg potatoes
3 fl.oz/85 ml cream
3 oz/75g butter
seasoning to taste

1. Peel and boil potatoes and swede.
2. Drain off water, add butter to the vegetables, season well and mash.
3. Keep hot in dish.
4. Pour cream into pan and warm gently.
5. Make holes in the vegetables with a skewer and pour cream over.

BESS'S BROCCOLI

Oven necessary
Serves 4   Wind force: 3
Preparation & cooking time: 55 minutes

1 lb/½ kg broccoli
3 oz/75g Cheddar cheese
1 oz/25g butter
1 × 5 oz/140g carton cream or yoghurt
1 level teaspoon caster sugar
½ level teaspoon paprika
½ level teaspoon salt
4 level tablespoons toasted breadcrumbs

1. Clean broccoli, grate cheese.
2. Place broccoli in buttered oven dish.
3. Mix cream or yoghurt with sugar, salt and paprika.
4. Cover broccoli with cream mixture. Sprinkle crumbs on top.
5. Bake for 45 minutes in moderate oven (325°F/160°C/Gas Mark 3).
6. Remove and cover with cheese, brown under grill or pop back into the oven for a minute or two.

GOOD OLD BUBBLE AND SQUEAK

Serves 4   Wind force: 4
Preparation & cooking time: 15 minutes

Of all vegetables cabbage seems to be the one most 'left over'. This is a tasty way to use it for lunch next day.

> *1 lb/½ kg left-over cooked potatoes*
> *1 lb/½ kg cooked cabbage*
> *1 onion*
> *seasoning*
> *1 oz/25g butter*
> *dash paprika*
> *1 egg*

1. Mash potatoes, chop cabbage well. Mix the two together and season.
2. Add paprika, mix in.
3. Chop onion, and fry in butter in pan.
4. Add onion to the potato mixture and stir in, add egg to bind together.
5. Drop spoonfuls of the mixture into the pan and fry, turning till a golden brown. Add a little more butter to pan if necessary.

☆

Potatoes roast best in poultry fat, particularly goose, if possible.

☆

MORE IDEAS

Wind force: up to 3 at least

Leeks Cut 1½ lb/¾ kg leeks into squares and place in pan with 1½ oz/40g butter. Put on lid. Cook very gently 10–15 minutes. Shake now and then. Season to taste. Add small pinch fennel seeds.

Spinach Cook in its own water, press out excess water when ready and add 3 tablespoons single cream, some nutmeg and seasoning. Add a small squeeze garlic purée and reheat, turning gently.

Swede Mash 2 lb/1 kg with 6 rashers cooked bacon, chopped finely. Add 2 tablespoons butter, a dash of cream and seasoning. Reheat.

Courgettes Slice, dip in egg and breadcrumbs and fry.

Cauliflower Au gratin – make with condensed celery soup and half quantity of milk plus 2 oz/50g grated cheese. Add bacon crisply fried; and (if desired) flaked crab meat or shrimps.

Mushrooms Can be fried with garlic or sautéed in brandy and butter.

Broad beans Are nice with nuts. Heat a tablespoon butter in a pan with 1 teaspoon lemon juice, 2 fl.oz/55 ml chicken stock and seasoning. Add 1 lb/½ kg beans and simmer about 10 minutes shaking now and then. Sauté 2 oz/50g nuts (hazel or almonds) in a tablespoon butter for 3 minutes. Stir in a squeeze of garlic purée and add all to the beans.

Cooked potatoes Toss 1 lb/½ kg cooked potatoes in 3 tablespoons butter with 1½ tablespoons sugar. When browning, turn low and toss continually till thickly coated.

Finally

● Add one-cup soups, made up to a fairly thick consistency, to various vegetables such as cooked beans, cabbage or celery to make them interesting.

● Add croûtons, breadcrumbs, peas, bacon or ham to leeks, cauliflower, and beans of all kinds to make a change.

Salads

Though not usually popular in cold and windy weather there are some salads which are tasty and filling and have the advantage of being easy to prepare early and keep.

It is good, too, to have something slightly different to your normal fare and so I include a few which may be new to you.

Seafood salads are particularly good if you happen to be anywhere in Brittany or the south-west of Britain or Eire where fish and shellfish are easily obtainable and excellent. The Channel Islands, a wonderful sailing area, are rich in seafoods.

Don't forget to cook extra potatoes, rice or pasta if you are planning a salad next day.

The white radishes mentioned in the vegetable chapter are more and more readily obtainable and, as well as being good in salads, can be added to sandwiches or Chinese dishes to give a crunchy texture.

Chinese leaves are now widely available and often keep better than lettuce. They are an excellent substitute for it in salads, as well as in Chinese dishes or cooked lightly as a vegetable.

I was given the second recipe in this chapter, Delta Salad, many years ago by the chef of the Delta Hotel in Vlaardingen near Rotterdam. It is unusual and quite delicious.

LIGHT LUNCH SALAD

Serves 4　　　　　　　　　　　　　Wind force: 2
Preparation time: 15 minutes

4 large bananas
lemon juice to coat
½ lb/225g green grapes
8 tablespoons muesli
8 tablespoons yoghurt

1. Pip grapes, slice bananas and coat with lemon juice.
2. Mix bananas and grapes. Place in four dishes.
3. Sprinkle on muesli and top with yoghurt.

If bad weather creeps up on you this can quickly be made up as a nutritious and satisfying stand-by meal.

☆

For a handy grape pipper unbend a paper clip, push end into a cork, make small loop in other end and use as a hook.

☆

72

DELTA SALAD

Serves 4   Wind force: 3
Preparation & cooking time: 15 minutes

1 medium celeriac root
1 apple
scant ½ pt/285 ml double or whipping cream
20 segments mandarin oranges (fresh or
*   tinned)*
seasoning to taste
½ teaspoon curry powder, if required

1. Peel celeriac and rough grate or cut into julienne strips.
2. Cook in salted boiling water for 2 minutes. Drain well.
3. Rinse in cold water to cool.
4. Peel and rough grate or cut apple into julienne strips.
5. Whip cream until thickly dropping from spoon.
6. Add apple, orange segments (stripped of pith if fresh), seasoning and celeriac to cream and mix well.

MARION'S SALAD

Serves 3–4   Wind force: 3
Preparation time: 10 minutes

3 red apples
7 oz/175g tin ham and pork luncheon meat
½ cucumber or 3 sticks celery
large handful of raisins
2 tomatoes
mayonnaise to mix
lettuce
paprika

1. Wash apples and cut into cubes, leaving skin on. Leave in acidulated or salted water until required.
2. Wash and cut celery or cucumber into pieces to match apples.

3. Wipe and cube tomatoes. Cube meat.
4. Line a dish with lettuce leaves.
5. Mix raisins and mayonnaise together and add to other ingredients, first patting the apples dry. Pile onto the lettuce. Sprinkle with a little paprika.
6. Cover with plastic film and leave in safe, cool place till required. Serve with crusty rolls, french bread or granary bread.

☆

Stand peeled, sliced onions in cold water for
ten minutes to make digetible to eat raw.

☆

THREE BEAN SALAD

Serves 4   Wind force 7
Preparation and cooking time: 5 minutes – if you feel up to it...

1 tin butter beans, drained
1 tin black-eyed peas/beans, drained
1 tin red kidney beans, drained
1 bottle salad dressing of your choice
half-tsp dried coriander

1. Mix the beans together in a bowl. Mix in the coriander.
2. Add as much of the dressing as required to coat all the beans well.

   Serve with a salad and left-over cold meat or a tin of cold ham or tongue.

☆

Milton added to water in which you wash
fruit and vegetables helps guard against
gastric problems. Rinse in fresh water
before drying off.

☆

HAM PIGS

Serves 4   Wind force: 4
Preparation time: 10 minutes

8 oz/225g curd cheese or Quark
seasoning to taste
2 teaspoons curry powder
1 box cress, lettuce or watercress
12 slices cooked ham

1. Mix cheese with curry powder and seasoning.
2. Add cress (chopped with scissors), lettuce or watercress to taste.
3. Mix well and divide between the ham slices.
4. Roll the slices up with the filling.
   Serve on lettuce leaves with more cress or watercress to garnish.

☆

A drop or two of Milton will remove stains from hard plastic cups and plates.

☆

STUFFED TOMATO

Serves 4   Wind force: 4
Preparation time: 10 minutes

4 large tomatoes
4 oz/100g cream cheese
1/2 oz/15g butter
chives
1 tablespoon milk
large pinch paprika

1. Cut tops off the tomatoes and scoop out the flesh. Chop the chives.
2. Mix together the other ingredients and add tomato flesh.
3. Spoon mixture back into the shells, top with the lids.
4. Fork the edges of the filling to make it pretty.
   Serve on a bed of lettuce.

NUTTY FRUIT SALAD

Serves 4   Wind force: 4
Pre-cook eggs then
preparation time: 20 minutes

Salad
10 oz/275g left-over cold cooked rice
8 hard boiled eggs
2 oz/50g raisins
2 oz/50g pecans or almonds
2 oz/50g spring onions
2 oranges

Dressing
2 fl.oz/55 ml orange juice
1 dessertspoon sugar
pinch salt

1. Clean and chop spring onions, peel and slice oranges across into rings.
2. Peel and slice eggs.
3. Place all ingredients into a bowl and mix gently.
4. Mix together dressing ingredients and pour over salad.

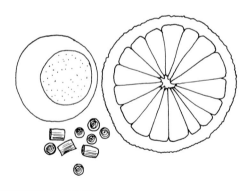

☆

Dangle unopened (or well corked) bottles of wine in mesh bags over the side in the sea to cool in hot weather.

☆

FURTHER IDEAS

Wind force: choose to suit up to 4
(higher than this it is unlikely
that salad will appeal)

• A platter of shellfish of your choice.

• A platter of continental sausages and cold meats, such as garlic sausage, salami, bierwurst, liver sausage, ham, tongue, smoked ham.

• A platter of assorted cheeses.

Garnish the above with sliced gherkins, flower radishes, water-lily tomatoes, cress etc. Serve with salads, seasoned to taste, as follows:

• Peas, celery, bean sprouts, cabbage, green pepper as available with mayonnaise or french dressing to coat.

• Thin sliced cabbage, nuts of choice, raisins, french dressing.

• Thin shredded carrots with cabbage or lettuce and nuts.

• Curried eggs with lettuce and thinly sliced onion.

• Noodles with raisins, pine nuts or salted peanuts, coated in mayonnaise.

• Avocado pear, mango, walnuts and raisins on lettuce bed with french dressing.

• Tomatoes, onion sprinkled with basil.

• Sliced cucumber in coconut milk.

• Diced potatoes, finely diced onion, mayonnaise, paprika with diced apple if desired.

• Cole slaw: thinly sliced cabbage, shredded carrots, sliced onion, diced or grated apple, handful of raisins, mayonnaise.

Sprouting seeds and beans You can use any variety such as mung beans, alfalfa, fenugreek etc., but do not mix them as they grow at different rates. The seeds and beans may be bought in packets from health food shops.

Take a glass (or transparent plastic) jar and add about a tablespoon of seeds. Wet them thoroughly and leave 15 minutes, then drain well. Place a piece of clean cloth or muslin, a piece of net curtain or even a piece of old tights over the top of the jar. Keep firmly in place with a rubber band. Keep out of the sun. Wet twice each day, tipping out the water at once. In 3 or 4 days the seeds will have sprouted and may be added to any meal to give a lovely crunchy texture.

The Sweet Course

Often while on holiday it is nicest to finish off a meal with fresh fruit or biscuits and cheese but it is also good to ring the changes now and then by producing a super sweet course, specially when there are children with you.

Since it is unlikely anyone would bother with sweets in bad weather unless they were pre-made I have not indicated a wind force but all are quickly or simply made.

Rice Pudding in a Vacuum Flask Using your favourite recipe (or for basic rice pudding recipe see Basic Recipes chapter) put the ingredients into a wide-necked vacuum flask and cover with boiling milk. Leave overnight, sealed, then quickly finish off the next day by heating (if desired), sprinkling with sugar and nutmeg and popping it under the grill for a moment or two to melt the sugar. The pudding can be eaten cold as it comes from the flask. It will not have the skin which baked rice pudding has, but it is otherwise much the same. Raisins or jam may be added.

APPLES AND CAMEMBERT

Serves 4
Preparation time: 5 minutes

4 crisp eating apples
4 wedges Camembert cheese

Give each person the apple and cheese on a plate with a knife and let them slice and eat the fruit and cheese for themselves. It makes a pleasant change from biscuits and cheese.

INSTANT TRIFLE

Serves 4
Preparation time: 5 minutes

4 thick slices swiss roll or stale cake
1 × 7½ oz/190g tin fruit to suit
4 tablespoons sherry
1 tin ready-made custard
1 × 10 oz/275g tin cream
chocolate shavings (optional)
nibbed nuts (optional)

1. In individual bowls place 1 slice swiss roll.
2. Pour a tablespoon of sherry over each.
3. Spoon over some fruit and a little juice.
4. Divide the tin of custard between each dish.
5. Add the cream and smooth over.
6. Sprinkle on some chocolate shavings or nibbed nuts if desired, and serve.

GOOSEBERRY FOOL
From *How to Cheat at Cooking*

Serves 4
Preparation time: 5 minutes plus 2–3 hours standing time

1 × 15 oz/425g tin gooseberries
½ pt/285 ml double cream

1. Drain gooseberries and mash to a pulp.
2. Whip cream and blend with the gooseberries.
3. Pour into a dish and chill (if possible) or keep cool for 2–3 hours.

TARTED UP SEMOLINA

Serves 2
Preparation & cooking time: 8 minutes

> *1 oz/25g butter*
> *1 oz/25g ground almonds*
> *2 oz/50g raisins*
> *½ teaspoon cinnamon*
> *1 × 16 oz/450g tin semolina (or see Basic*
>   *Recipes chapter)*
> *2 tablespoons soft brown sugar*

1. Heat butter and add ground almonds, raisins and spice.
2. Cook, stirring for about 2 minutes.
3. Stir in semolina and allow to heat through.
4. Pour into dish, sprinkle with sugar and flash grill for 1 minute.

> ☆
> *Ground ginger is good added to tinned milk puddings.*
> ☆

MOUTHWATERING OMELETTE

Make one omelette at a time
Preparation & cooking time:
about 7 minutes for one

1. Prepare an omelette as usual (make enough mixture for the crew to be fed, then cook individually).
2. Before serving each omelette tip into the pan and heat with the folded omelette the following (for each person):

> *2½ fl.oz/70 ml white or red wine*
> *1 heaped teaspoon Barbados sugar, honey or*
>   *similar*
> *pinch cinnamon*

3. When the whole is hot serve the omelette and pour sauce from pan over the top.

SCOTTISH CRANACHAN

Serves 6
Preparation & cooking time: 15 minutes

Make this just before you want to eat it, but the oatmeal may be grilled beforehand.

> *1 level tablespoon clear honey*
> *3 tablespoons whisky*
> *8 oz/225g raspberries (fresh if possible, or well*
>   *drained tin)*
> *2 oz/50g medium oatmeal*
> *½ pt/285 ml whipping or double cream*

1. Toast oatmeal gently under the grill, stirring occasionally till pale gold. Cool.
2. Whip cream till it holds its shape.
3. Add whisky and honey.
4. Add cooled oatmeal.
5. Arrange most of the raspberries in individual dishes. Reserve a few for decoration. Spoon oatmeal mixture on top. Decorate with the remaining raspberries.

PLEASE YOURSELF FRUIT SALAD

Serves as many as you wish
Preparation time: 10 minutes

> *at least 4 fruits of your choice*
> *sugar to taste*
> *4 tablespoons brandy or wine*

1. Clean, peel and slice any fruit you wish, mixing together.
2. Add brandy or wine and stir in.
3. Cover with plastic film till required, giving time to marinade. Add sugar if desired.

Serve with cream, yoghurt or, if available, crème fraîche or Quark.

If using fruit that will discolour such as apples or bananas use at least one acidic fruit (pineapple, orange or grapefruit) to preserve the colour. Bananas are best added at the last minute as they go soft if left unzipped.

OLD FAITHFUL GINGERNUT PUDDING

Serves 4
Preparation time: 10 minutes

2 chunks stem ginger (preserved in heavy
*   syrup)*
1 tablespoon dry sherry
5 fl.oz/140 ml double cream (or a tin)
16 ginger snap biscuits

1. Whip cream fairly stiffly.
2. Chop ginger finely, add to the cream.
3. Add sherry to the cream and ginger.
4. Sandwich the ginger snaps together with part of the cream mixture.
5. Lay on a plate standing on their edges. Cover with the rest of the cream mixture.
6. Decorate with a little extra ginger.

☆

To preserve fresh ginger, lemon or orange peel, place in jar, cover with gin, sherry, vinegar or similar. Add a little sugar to the peel. Screw on top and shake. Top up and use as required.

☆

WAIT AWHILE CHOC POTS

Serves 6
Preparation & cooking time: 10 minutes plus 2 hours standing time

4 oz/100g plain dark chocolate
2 eggs
5 fl.oz/140 ml yoghurt

1. Melt chocolate over water. Separate eggs.
2. Add yolks to chocolate and mix in.
3. Beat whites until stiff.
4. Add 4 oz/100g of the yoghurt to the chocolate mixture.

5. Fold in egg whites.
6. Put the mixture into 6 dishes and swirl rest of yoghurt over the top of each.
7. Leave in cool place to set for 2 hours.

BANOFFIE PIE

Make any amount to suit number of people
Preparation and cooking time: 15 minutes, plus 2 hours to boil the condensed milk.

digestive biscuits, crushed
melted butter to bind biscuits
1 large tin condensed milk, boiled to a toffee
*   consistency*
sliced bananas
whipped or tinned cream & instant coffee, mixed
cinnamon

1. Mix biscuits and butter. Press into a tin.
2. Slice bananas and place on top.
3. Pour prepared condensed milk over bananas.
4. Mix cream and coffee to taste. Spread over milk.
5. Sprinkle on cinnamon. Chill if possible.

BANANA BUTTERSCOTCH PUDDING
From *How to Cheat at Cooking*

Serves 4
Preparation time: 7 minutes

1 packet butterscotch instant whip
4 bananas
4 digestive biscuits
4 tablespoons nibbed or chopped nuts

1. Mix instant whip according to instructions on packet.
2. Crush the digestive biscuits.
3. Peel and slice the bananas crossways.
4. Stir the whip into the bananas, add biscuit crumbs.
5. Pour into 4 dishes and top with nuts.

MELT IN THE MOUTH MARS ICE

Serves as many as you wish
Preparation & cooking time: 5 minutes

Take 1 Mars Bar and a portion of ice cream for each person. Melt the Mars Bars, pour over the ice cream and serve at once.

NOTHING

Serves 4
Preparation & cooking time: 15 minutes plus 1 hour standing time

1 × 15 oz/425g cold evaporated milk
1 jelly of your choice
¼ pt/140 ml boiling water

1. Whip evaporated milk till thick and doubled in bulk.
2. Dissolve jelly in boiling water.
3. Whisk jelly into evaporated milk.
4. Pour into a dish and leave to set for an hour. Rewhisk when almost set.

The title arose from the chorus 'What's for pudding, Mummy?' 'Nothing.'

PEACHY IDEAS

Basis
1 tin peach halves, or fresh peaches, skinned (2 halves per person)

● Halve the peaches, lay in dish, pour over white wine, marinade for 3–4 hours.

● Lay 2 half peaches in a dish, cut side up. Mix some stale cake crumbs with sherry, pile into peach halves and spoon thick cream on top.

● Cut a chocolate swiss roll into 4 and lay in bowls. Sprinkle on sherry and lay a peach half on top, cut side down. Top with whipped cream and nibbed or chopped nuts.

● Lay peach halves on flat dish, top with whipped cream and soft brown sugar. Place under grill for a moment or two only.

MORE IDEAS

● Bought meringue baskets or nests, filled with stale cake crumbs mixed with sherry and topped with cream.

● Bought meringue nests, filled with fresh fruit and topped with cream. Drizzle over liqueur as required.

● Bought meringue baskets filled with tinned custard into which has been folded 1 tablespoon sherry. Top with cream and chocolate curls.

● Bought meringue nests filled with made-up instant pudding and topped with cream.

● Bought meringue nests filled with ice cream and fruit. Top with butterscotch or chocolate sauce.

● Apples or pears poached in red or white wine with sugar.

● Bought chocolate cases may also be used to contain fillings.

☆
Place a cube of bread in sugar to keep sugar dry. Replace regularly.
☆

Savoury and Sweet Sauces and Dressings

There are now many and varied sauces to be had in bottles and tins which are quick and tasty but you may find the following *easily made* recipes handy. I have again left out the wind force factor as it is unlikely one would be fiddling with sauces if the weather had turned nasty.

BASIC WHITE SAUCE

Preparation & cooking time: 10 minutes

This can easily be adapted as the basis for several sauces by mixing one of the additions listed below after or during cooking.

A roux is a mixture of melted butter and flour (usually on a one to one ratio); it is the basis of many sauces and is used as a thickening for stews etc.

2 oz/50g butter or margarine
2 oz/50g flour
1 pt/570 ml milk
seasoning to taste

1. Melt the butter in a pan.
2. Add flour and beat till smooth over a low flame – about 3 minutes – stirring all the time.
3. Gradually add a little milk and stir in, then repeat. This way you should not have any lumps.
4. When the roux is smooth and easily stirred you can pour in the rest of the milk.
5. Cook, stirring, till the mixture is combined and of a consistency to coat the back of a wooden spoon. Season to taste.

To make thicker or thinner as required use more or less roux to the pint of milk but keep the butter to flour ratio the same. Alternatively add or leave out some milk as desired.

To thicken a thin stew prepare a roux by mixing the butter and flour together with a fork. Then slide the mixture into the stew down the side of the pan, stirring all the time. Cook for about 3 minutes to cook flour. Add more roux till desired consistency is reached.

VARIATIONS

Cheese sauce: Grate 2 oz/50g to 3 oz/75g strong tasting cheese and add to white sauce when milk has been incorporated; stir over a low heat till cheese is melted.

Mustard sauce: Mix about a dessertspoon of dry mustard (this really should be added in small quantities until desired taste has been achieved) with a little water, then stir into the white sauce.

Onion sauce: Finely chop a large onion and fry gently for a moment or two till transparent in the butter or margarine *before* adding the flour. Continue as before.

Parsley sauce: Finely chop enough parsley (approximately 2–3 tablespoons) to give a good green colour to the completed white sauce. Stir in well.

Sweet white sauce: Make the roux a little thicker and add sugar to taste. Stir over low heat till melted. You may then add essences for flavour, or a little whisky, brandy, rum or liqueur to taste.

Cornflour sauce: Cornflour may be used to make a white sauce in place of plain flour. This is often better for sweet sauces. If using cornflour reserve some milk to mix with it before adding to the hot milk – no fat is required. Add sugar and other flavourings to taste as above.

APPLE SAUCE

Preparation & cooking time: 10 minutes

1 lb/450g cooking or sharp apples
1 oz/25g butter
a little sugar to taste

1. Peel, core and slice or chop the apples.
2. Put them into a pan and cook them gently with a tablespoon of water until soft, breaking down with a wooden spoon.
3. Beat the apple purée till smooth. Add the butter and beat in.
4. Add sugar to taste and fold in. Cool.

BARBECUE SAUCE

Preparation & cooking time: 5 minutes

½ oz/15g margarine
2 tablespoons lemon juice
1 teaspoon vinegar
1 tablespoon tomato purée
1 tablespoon brown sauce
2 tablespoons honey

1. Heat all the ingredients together, stirring till blended and hot.
2. Pour over meat, and baste with the sauce while cooking.
   Try with pork chops or sausages.

FRENCH DRESSING

Preparation time: 2 minutes

Try this with hot boiled potatoes as well as salads.

1 tablespoon wine vinegar
3 tablespoons oil of your choice
squeeze of lemon juice
½ teaspoon dry mustard
seasoning to taste

Put all the ingredients into a screw topped jar and put the lid on securely. Shake hard. Add herbs as required.

MAYONNAISE

Preparation time: 10–15 minutes

This is best beaten by hand with a wooden spoon but it is hard work and is possible with a hand or rotary whisk.

¼ pt/140 ml olive oil (or half olive–half
sunflower oil)
½ tablespoon vinegar (wine vinegar is good)
1 egg yolk
½ teaspoon dry mustard
seasoning to taste

1. Stir the egg yolk and mustard in a deep bowl to break down and mix.
2. Stir in the oil, *drop by drop*, beating all the time. You will find the mixture becomes thicker and thicker and when half the oil has been added it should be very thick.
3. Now begin to beat in the vinegar, alternating with the oil. This *must* be done in slow degrees but not drop by drop. If you rush it the mixture will thin and perhaps separate.
4. When all is complete add seasoning to taste.
   If the mixture should curdle then beat another egg yolk separately and beat the curdled mixture into it drop by drop.

EASY SALAD DRESSING

Preparation time: 5 minutes

This is much quicker than mayonnaise but does not, of course, taste the same. None the less it is a good substitute if required.

> *½ pt/285 ml whipping cream*
> *½ teaspoon dry mustard*
> *1 fl.oz/30 ml vinegar or lemon juice*
> *seasoning to taste*

1. Beat the cream and mustard to mayonnaise consistency while adding the vinegar slowly.
2. Season to taste.
3. Add herbs or spices to this if desired.

Tartare sauce is made by adding some *very* finely chopped spring onions and a tablespoon of finely chopped fresh tarragon or parsley to either of the above dressings.

TOMATO SAUCE

Preparation & cooking time: 35 minutes

Try with fish or sausages

> *1 oz/25g butter*
> *1 oz/25g flour*
> *1½ lb/675g (or a very large tin) tomatoes*
> *1 teaspoon basil*
> *seasoning to taste*
> *2 teaspoons soft brown sugar*

1. Melt butter and cook flour for a moment.
2. Add rest of ingredients and bring to boil, stirring well.
3. Simmer roughly half an hour.
4. Squash tomatoes to distribute. Sieve the sauce to remove skin.
5. Check seasoning.

YOGHURT DRESSING

Preparation time: 5 minutes

> *2 fl.oz/55 ml plain yoghurt (Greek is good)*
> *1 tablespoon thick mayonnaise*
> *1 teaspoon lemon juice*
> *dash Worcester sauce*
> *1 tablespoon chopped chives or spring onions*
> *seasoning*

Mix all ingredients thoroughly then serve.
  Try with salads or add to sandwiches. Pile on a baked potato.

JEAN'S HOMEMADE YOGHURT

Preparation time: 5 minutes then 24 hours

This makes a thick, slightly sweet yoghurt that is useful in emergencies.

> *12 oz/350g tin evaporated milk*
> *6 tablespoons powdered milk*
> *6 tablespoons good commercial yoghurt*

Mix together all ingredients, put into jars with lids on and leave overnight in warm place to thicken.

CARAMEL SAUCE

Preparation & cooking time: 10 minutes

> *½ oz/15g butter*
> *2–3 drops vanilla essence*
> *4 oz/100g soft brown sugar*
> *7½ oz/190g tin evaporated milk*

1. Put all ingredients in pan and cook gently, stirring, for about 5–8 minutes. Remove from heat.
2. Beat for a moment until glossy, then serve hot or cold.

Bread, Biscuits, Scones and Cakes

An oven is necessary for most of the following goodies and they are not likely to be made in heavy weather (though no doubt on larger boats it would not be too difficult).

However, it is useful to be able to make bread (and the recipe included is very easy) when you are getting low and to produce some tasty bites for visitors or a deserving crew. Some of the baking can be done at home and brought on board and most of the recipes given keep well. Biscuits on board are marvellous stop-gaps and disappear with swift regularity on our boat.

ONE CUP MALT LOAF

Oven necessary   Wind force: in harbour
Preparation & cooking time: 10 minutes, then overnight, then 1 hour

1 cup All-bran
1 cup sugar
1 cup mixed fruit
1 cup milk
1 cup self-raising flour

1. Mix all ingredients together and leave covered in a bowl overnight.
2. Bake in a greased loaf tin in a moderate oven (350°F/180°C/Gas Mark 4) for an hour, turning several times. Test with a skewer to make sure the cake is cooked.

When cool, slice and eat with butter.

The size of the cup does not matter as long as the same cup is used for all the ingredients. I used an 8 oz/225g cup.

OATMEAL MUNCHIES

Oven necessary   Wind force: in harbour
Preparation & cooking time: 25 minutes

1/2 lb/225g short crust pastry (see Basic Recipes chapter)

1. Line a swiss roll tin with pastry, rolled fairly thin.
2. Brush with raspberry jam heated with a little water.

Filling
4 oz/100g fine oats
4 oz/100g demerara or soft brown sugar
4 oz/100g butter or margarine
6 drops almond essence

1. Melt butter, add sugar and oats. Mix well.
2. Add essence and mix. Pour onto pastry and smooth.
3. Bake in a hot oven (425°F/220°C/Gas Mark 7) for 10–15 minutes until golden brown. (Watch for burning.)

Cut into squares when cold.

☆

Covering jams, marmalades etc., with melted candle wax (then placing plastic film over top) helps preserve them if you are leaving them unused for a time.

☆

SCOTS PANCAKES

Preparation & cooking time: Wind force: 2
20 minutes

> *8 oz/225g self-raising flour*
> *½ teaspoon salt*
> *1 tablespoon sugar*
> *1 teaspoon cream of tartar*
> *1 egg*
> *10 fl.oz/285 ml milk*

1. Mix dry ingredients together. Add egg and beat well.
2. Add enough milk to give a soft dropping consistency.
3. Heat a frying pan and rub with buttery paper.
4. Drop a tablespoon mixture into pan. It should hold 4 at once.
5. Cook over medium heat until top bubbles break.
6. Flip over with a knife and cook other side till golden.

   Raise heat if the bubbles break before the underside is golden, lower if too brown underneath. The pancakes must be put immediately into a clean tea towel, folded over, to cool. Eat as soon as possible with butter and jam or honey.

NEVER FAIL FRUIT CAKE

Oven necessary   Wind force: 3
Preparation & cooking time: 1 hour 45 minutes

> *1 lb/450g mixed fruit or sultanas*
> *8 oz/225g caster sugar*
> *water to boil*
> *10 oz/275g flour*
> *8 oz/225g soft margarine or butter*
> *3 eggs*
> *pinch salt*
> *1 teaspoon baking powder*
> *1 teaspoon each lemon, vanilla, almond*
>   *flavouring*

1. Put fruit into a pan and cover with water. Boil 3 minutes then strain.
2. Put fruit into basin with chopped margarine, sugar and flavouring.
3. Stir with knife till margarine and sugar are dissolved.
4. Leave to cool for a while, then add beaten eggs and sifted flour, salt and baking powder.
5. Bake in a 7in square tin (18cm) in moderate oven (325°F/170°C/Gas Mark 3) for 1½ hours, turning now and then, till skewer comes out clean.

HEDGEHOG

Preparation & cooking time: Wind force: 3
25 minutes plus 2 hours to set

10 oz/275g sweet biscuits
4 oz/100g sugar
4 oz/100g unsalted butter
½ oz/15g cocoa
1 large egg
few drops vanilla essence
4 oz/100g chopped walnuts (optional)

1. Line a 7in × 11in (18cm × 27cm) tin with greaseproof paper.
2. Crush biscuits in plastic bag.
3. Break nuts and chop. Beat egg.
4. Mix the nuts and biscuits.
5. Heat sugar, butter and cocoa until butter melts.
6. Add egg. Stir over gentle heat for 2–3 minutes until thick. Add to biscuit mix and stir well together.
7. Press well into tin. Leave 2 hours in cool place to set. Cut into small squares when quite hard.

BARBARA'S BISCUITS

Oven necessary   Wind force: 3
Preparation & cooking time: 30 minutes

4 oz/100g flour
3 oz/75g margarine
2 oz/50g sugar
few drops vanilla essence

1. Mix all ingredients together till smooth then roll into walnut sized pieces with fingers. Flatten into rounds and place on baking tray.
2. Bake 20 minutes in a moderate oven (350°F/ 180°C/Gas Mark 4) till golden. Remove from tray and cool.

MAUREEN'S ORANGE OR LEMON BISCUITS

Oven necessary   Wind force: 3
Preparation & cooking time: 30 minutes

5 oz/125g self-raising flour
4 oz/100g margarine
5 oz/125g sugar
grated rind of 1 orange or lemon

1. Mix all ingredients together. Shape into walnut sized lumps.
2. Flatten slightly and place on baking tray.
3. Bake 15 minutes in a moderate oven (350°F/ 180°C/Gas Mark 4).
4. Sprinkle with some sugar while hot.

JANET'S PERFECT CORN BREAD

Preparation & cooking time: approx 45 minutes

1 cup plain flour
quarter cup sugar
4 tsp baking powder
three-quarter tsp salt
1 cup yellow cornmeal (NOT cornflour)
2 eggs
1 cup milk
quarter cup soft margarine

1. Mix all the dry ingredients. Add the eggs, milk and margarine.
2. Use a whisk and beat until just smooth. Don't overdo it.
3. Pour into a greased 9-in square tin. Bake at 425°F/220°C/gas mark 7 for 20-25 minutes until cooked through when tested with a skewer.
4. Cut into squares.

This is delicious served hot with butter and jam, and also good with cheese for lunch or with bacon and eggs for breakfast. It also goes well with spicy Mexican dishes.

MARY'S QUICK BOAT BREAD

Oven necessary
Makes a 1 lb/450g loaf   Wind force: 3
Preparation & cooking time: 1 hour
(plus up to an hour rising time)

1 lb/450g wholewheat flour
1 oz/25g packet direct mix yeast
1 heaped teaspoon salt
1 egg
½ dessertspoon brown sugar, molasses or
*   honey*
½ pt/285 ml water

1. Heat water to blood heat.
2. Grease baking tin well.
3. Place flour in bowl sifting a little with fingers, add salt and yeast and stir.
4. Break in egg and sweetening, top up with water, stirring and adding a little at a time. You may need a little more or less water, depending on your flour. The mixture when well mixed should be moist but not sticky.
5. Turn out onto floured surface, flour hands and knead for five minutes.
6. Shape and put into bread tin, cover with greased polythene bag and set in warm place till well risen (about ½–1 hour).
7. Pre-heat oven to hot (450°F/230°C/Gas Mark 8).
8. Cook 20–25 minutes. Turn off oven and leave another 20 minutes without opening door. Turn out loaf to cool on rack. It should sound hollow when base is tapped sharply.

Keep all utensils and ingredients warm when making bread, use a wooden board for kneading.

My boat oven cools quickly so I leave the power on low for second half of cooking. I turn loaf several times as well for even baking.

The following is half way between bread and scone and easy to make. It is a godsend in an emergency.

JEAN'S AUSTRALIAN DAMPER

Oven necessary
Serves 6   Wind force: 4
Preparation & cooking time: 30 minutes

14 oz/400g self-raising flour
1½ teaspoons salt
4 oz/100g butter
4 fl.oz/115 ml milk
4 fl.oz/115 ml water
extra flour

1. Sift flour and salt into a bowl. Rub in butter till mixture is like evenly sized breadcrumbs.
2. Make a well in centre, add milk and water all at once.
3. Mix lightly with sharp knife in a cutting motion.
4. Knead lightly and shape into a 6in (15cm) circle.
5. Place on oven tray and with knife cut 3 slits across the top ½ in. (1cm) deep, to give 6 portions.
6. Brush top with milk, sift extra flour over if desired.
7. Bake in a hot oven (475°F/240°C/Gas Mark 9) for 10 minutes until golden.
8. Reduce heat to moderate (375°F/240°C/Gas Mark 5) for a further 15 minutes. Turn in the oven now and then for an even bake.

☆
When using dried yeast only use half quantity of that required in a recipe using fresh.
☆

Relax with some Nibbles

When in harbour people are always dropping in from other boats for a chat or to compare notes. Life is easy-going and there is always time for a drink and nibble.

The following few nibbles are easy and a bit unusual which makes them interesting. Because they will normally be made beforehand or while in harbour I have omitted the wind force factor.

The two nut nibble recipes will keep for a week or two.

AUSTRALIAN PEANUT SURPRISE

Preparation time: 10 minutes

Make before you go and put into an airtight container.

11 oz/340g Quaker Oat Krunchies
1 × 1½ pt/825 ml packet cream of chicken
*   soup*
1½ lb/675g salted peanuts
1 × 1½ pt/825 ml packet french onion soup
1 teaspoon dry mustard
2 dessertspoons curry powder
3 fl.oz/85 ml (about ⅓ cup) warm oil

1. Heat oil a little.
2. Mix all the dry ingredients together thoroughly.
3. Add and mix in the warm oil. Store in airtight container. The quantity fills a large sweet jar, which can be gleaned from a sweet shop.

Different and delicious as nibbles to serve with drinks.

SHIRLEY'S SPICY ALMONDS

Preparation & cooking time: 10 minutes

Make before you go and store in airtight container. This only makes a small quantity.

1 fl.oz/25 ml good quality oil
4 oz/100g flaked almonds
½ teaspoon salt
1 teaspoon curry powder
tiny pinch chilli powder and ground ginger

1. Heat the oil in a deep pan and add almonds.
2. Fry the almonds until golden, drain on kitchen paper.
3. Return to pan and sprinkle on the salt and spices, tossing well to coat. Leave to cool.

MORE IDEAS

● Bacon rind makes a lovely nibble if cut into small pieces and fried in a dry frying pan until crisp, turning frequently. Drain and cool on kitchen paper. Left-over pork or chicken skin can also be treated this way.

● Use dried marrowfat peas instead of nuts. Soak 4 oz/100g peas in cold water for a day. Drain and dry well. Fry the peas in fat, shaking gently, until crisp, about 5 minutes. Drain on kitchen paper and shake a little salt, garlic salt or celery salt on them.

● Cubes of white radish speared with cubes of Edam or Gouda cheese are delicious. Cheese and pickled onions are good too.

Utensils, Equipment and Ship's Stores

Your galley space will determine the equipment you can carry, but I have found the following to be basic and useful:

UTENSILS AND EQUIPMENT

1 fish slice
1 slotted metal spoon
1 measuring jug
1 whistling kettle
1 bottle opener/cork screw
1 hand held tin opener
1 deep sided frying pan with lid (or use a spatter guard)
1 small saucepan (milk pan is useful size)
1 pressure cooker (could double as large pan)
1 grill pan and rack
Knife sharpener (I use the skipper's tool sharpening stone)
1 grater/Mouli grater
1 small whisk
Sandwich toaster (Taste-T-Toast, if you can find one)
Vegetable peeler
Measuring cups, spoons, mini scales (depending on space)
If you can find them, a set of three-cornered, fit-together-on-one-burner pans are useful instead of some above.

A plastic 'shaker' to shake up sauce bases etc. saves mess.
1 wooden spoon
1 all-purpose large sharp knife
1 all-purpose small sharp knife
1 double-sided bread/chopping board
1 sieve/strainer
1 medium pan with lid
1 large pan with lid
1 pump action vacuum flask
1 pair kitchen scissors
2–3 skewers
Sugar, tea, coffee containers
Fire blanket and extinguisher

If you have an oven you will need:
1 oven thermometer (if no thermostat on oven)
1 bread baking tin
1 round baking tin
1 swiss roll tin
1 roasting tin
1 flat tray with small rim
Roasting bags

Household equipment
Small scrubbing brush
Paper towels
Matches
Cloths
Plastic film
Foil
Plastic food bags
Duster
Soap, liquid soap, washing powder
Washing-up liquid
Pegs, rope for drying washing
Scouring powder, bleach, ammonia
1 sponge cloth
Soap pads or stove cleaner
Toothpicks or cocktail sticks
Loo brush
Floor cloth
Plastic containers for all sorts of things
Fly killer or fly papers
Air freshener

Polishes, various as required (furniture, chrome, brass etc.)
Mosquito coils

Tableware
(Basic for 4 crew)
4 meat knives
4 tea knives
4 dessert forks
4 meat forks
4 dessert spoons
4 teaspoons
4 soup spoons
4 egg spoons (optional)
4 cups/mugs
4 large plates
4 small plates
4 deep bowls
1 large serving spoon
4 egg cups
1 milk jug, sugar bowl
1 teapot
Salt and pepper set
Butter dish
Nibble containers/plates
Salad dish, serving dish

If it is possible to stick rubber rings on the base of your plates this will prevent them slipping about. You can, in fact, buy crockery with rings already in place. Remember not to push your cup away from you when you are finished; it will tip over.

If you have room in the galley a salt water pump is useful.

A small Gaz stove is useful for emergencies as is a Gaz heater for winter.

SHIP'S STORES

It is impossible to tell individuals what they should have on board; tastes differ so much. I believe that, unless you are preparing for a long voyage or are departing for shores where certain items are either unobtainable or expensive, carrying a large number of tins and boxes is pointless. Store enough for immediate needs and emergencies and buy everything else fresh at your next port of call.

The list below gives a fairly comprehensive list of items that are useful in the stores locker; each sea-cook must choose for their own crew or family. Use the list as a check to make sure nothing has been forgotten.

TINNED GOODS

Soups

Have both condensed and
   ready-to-serve soups
   handy
Asparagus
Celery
Chicken
Consommé
Leek
Lentil
Lobster bisque
Mushroom
Onion
Scotch broth
Tomato
Vegetable

Juices

Grapefruit
Orange
Pineapple
Tomato
Vegetable
Ready mixed sauces,
   white/red wine, white
   sauce, etc.

Fish

Cockles
Crab
Mackerel
Mussels
Pilchards
Salmon
Sardines
Shrimps or prawns
Smoked oysters
Tuna
Anchovies – for garnish

Sweets and dairy

Butter
Condensed milk
Cream
Custard (ready-made)
Dried milk
Evaporated milk
Rice
Sago
Semolina
Steamed pudding
U.H.T. milk

Meat

Chicken in jelly
Chicken supreme
Chilli con carne
Chunky chicken
Corned beef
Curried beef
Curried chicken
Frankfurters
Ham
Hamburgers
Luncheon meat
Meatballs
Mince
Chopped pork and ham
Rolled pork
Sausages, various
Steak and kidney pie
Steak and kidney pudding
Stewing beef
Tongue

Vegetables

Artichoke hearts
Asparagus
Beans (kidney, baked,
   flageolet, butter,
   broad, french, black
   eyed etc.)
Carrots
Celeriac
Celery
Mushrooms
Peas
Peppers
Pimiento
Potatoes
Spanish rice
Sprouting seeds (mung,
   alfalfa, fenugreek etc.)
Sweetcorn
Tomatoes – juice, whole,
   purée

Fruit

Apple sauce
Apple slices
Apricots
Cherries
Chestnut purée
Creamed coconut and
   coconut milk
Gooseberries
Grapefruit
Mandarin oranges
Peaches
Pears
Plums
Pie fillings
Pineapple chunks, slices,
   crushed
Raspberries
Rhubarb
Strawberries
Unsweetened pineapple

☆

If your loo roll insists on unrolling at sea, remove from holder and put an elastic band round the roll. Replace roll on holder. When in use just push the band aside onto the holder and replace on roll when finished.

☆

DRY STORES

Aspic
Biscuits – chocolate, cheese, sweet and for dips
Breadcrumbs
Cakes
Cherries – glacé
Cereals
Chocolate – drinking, eating, cooking
Citric acid
Cocoa
Coconut, dessicated
Coffee
Cornflour
Crispbreads
Crisps
Custards – various
Flours – various
Fruits, various
Epsom salts
Garlic – dry, tube purée
Gelatine
Ground almonds
Ground rice
Herbs – dry, purée (see separate list)
Instant puddings
Jellies
Meringues
Milk powder

Muesli
Mustard
Nuts – almond, brazil, hazelnuts, peanuts, pecans, pine nuts, walnuts etc.
Oatmeal, fine, medium, coarse
Oats – rolled
Onions, dry
Pasta – various
Pepper, black and white
Peppers – dry
Potato – dry
Pulses – barley, beans, peas, lentils
Rice – various
Sago
Salt
Semolina
Stock cubes
Sosmix
Soups – one-cup, packet
Spices – various (see separate list)
Sugar – brown, white, caster, demerara, icing
Sweets
Tomato – tubes of purée
Tartaric acid
Vegetables – dried

Herbs

Basil (tomato, lamb)
Bay leaves (stews)
Chervil (salads, fish)
Dill seeds or tips (salads, fish, potato)
Fennel (fish)
Marjoram (lamb, pork)
Mixed herbs (beef, pork, stews)
Rosemary (lamb, stews)
Sage (stuffings, onions, fish)
Tarragon (salads, fish)
Thyme (stuffings, eggs, liver, bacon, fish)

Sauces and bottled stores

Anchovy essence
Chocolate spread
Chutneys
Essences – almond, lemon, vanilla, rum, peppermint etc.
Food colouring
Fruit juices
Gherkins, pickled onions
Honey
Jams – apricot, raspberry, strawberry etc.
Jellies – apple, mint, red currant, cranberry etc.
Lemon juice
Marmalade
Yeast extract & meat extract (Marmite, Bovril)

Meat and fish pastes
Peanut butter
Pickles and relishes
Oils, cooking
Olives
Sauces – apple, barbecue, brown, butterscotch, chilli (and paste), chocolate, french dressing, H.P., horseradish, mayonnaise, mint, oyster, salad cream, soya, sweet and sour, Tabasco, tomato, Worcester.
Soused herrings, cockles, mussels
Vinegars – various

Spices

Cardamom seeds or ground
Cayenne pepper
Chilli powder
Cinnamon sticks and ground
Cloves
Coriander seeds or ground
Cummin seeds or ground
Curry powder
Fenugreek seeds and ground
Five spice powder
Garam masala
Ginger root, stem, fresh, ground
Mixed spice
Nutmeg
Paprika
Turmeric

☆

It saves time and effort to put a little washing powder and nappy cleanser into a bucket each night, add water and dirty clothing Swish round and leave overnight. Next morning they are easily rinsed ready to hang out to dry.

☆

FRESH FOODS

Dairy, meat, fish
Bacon
Butter
Cheeses, various
Cold meats
Cream
Eggs
Fish
Margarine, lard
Meat
Meat pies etc.
Milk
Pâté
Sausages
Yoghurt

Bread, cakes etc.
Brown bread
Cakes
Chappatis
Crisps, nibbles
Granary bread
Pitta bread
Poppadoms
Prawn crackers for curries
Rye bread
Rolls, baps, croissants
White bread

**Fresh vegetables and
  salads**
Artichokes
Asparagus
Aubergines
Beans, various
Brussels sprouts
Cabbage
Carrots
Celery
Celeriac
Cress, watercress
Cucumber
Garlic
Ginger, fresh
Lettuce, Chinese leaves,
  endive
Mushrooms
Onions
Parsnips
Peas
Peppers
Potatoes
Pumpkin
Radishes, white radishes
Spring greens
Spring onions
Sweetcorn
Tomatoes
Turnip, swede

☆
*If you wish to keep eggs for a longish time
coat each with vaseline and pack well or
paint with varnish and turn frequently.*
☆

FROZEN FOODS

Fish fingers
Fruit
Hamburgers
Ice cream, sorbet

Meats
Ready-cooked meals
Sausages
Vegetables

FRESH FRUIT

Apples
Apricots
Avocados
Bananas
Grapefruit
Grapes
Kiwi fruit
Lemons

Nectarines
Oranges
Pears
Peaches
Pineapple
Plums
Soft fruit

LIQUOR & DRINKS

Liquor
Angostura bitters
Aquavit
Bacardi
Beer
Brandy
Campari
Cider
Dubonnet
Geneva gin
Gin
Guinness
Lager, Pils
Liqueurs
Pimms
Rum
Sherry
Vermouth – sweet and
dry
Whisky
Wines – red, white and
rosé

Mixers, soft drinks
Bitter lemon
Cola
Cordials
Fizzy drinks
Ginger ale
Ginger beer
Lemon, orange barley
water
Lemon, orange squash
Lemonade
Lime juice
Soda water
Tonic water
If you have room, an
aerating machine with
concentrates is useful.

Index